THE 7 LEVELS OF PRAYER

A Tested Formula for Approaching The Throne of Grace

THE 7 LEVELS OF PRAYER

Obtaining Uncommon Results in Uncommon Ways

Copyright @ 2015 by Victor Oludiran

All rights reserved. No part of this book may be produced, copied, or stored or transmitted in any form or by any means --graphic, electronic, or mechanical, including photocopying, recording, or information storage and retrieval system without the prior written permission of Licaim publishing, except when permitted by law.

Unless otherwise specified, all Scripture quotations in this book are from The Holy Bible, New King James Version. NKJV is public domain in the United States printed in 1987.

LICAIM PUBLISHING
915 Woodland Trail
Smyrna GA, 30080, USA
admin@licaim.org
www.licaim.org

ISBN-13:
978-1519238344

ISBN-10:
1519238347

Printed in the United States of America

THE 7 LEVELS OF PRAYER

DEDICATION

This book is dedicated to my spiritual parents, Bishop and Rev (Mrs) Sam Amao-Thomas, who fed me with the sincere milk of the word as a new believer, and taught me how to pray effective prayers. I thank and appreciate you sincerely for your love, and for making my divine connection with you a fruitful one.

ACKNOWLEDGMENTS

I acknowledge the following people who contributed to the editing, proofing and production of this book in one way or the other: Dr. Dejo Afolayan, Christina Enohnyaket, Yemi Oludiran, Bishop Henry Adekogbe, Apostle Tim Atunnise, and my lovely wife, Janet Oludiran. May God make it happen for you according to the desire of your heart, and reward your labor of love.

Contents

DEDICATION .... **II**

ACKNOWLEDGMENTS .... **III**

PREFACE .... **V**

INTRODUCTION **1**

CHAPTER 1
    LEVEL 1: PRAYER OF ASKING AND RECEIVING 7

CHAPTER 2
    LEVEL 2: PRAYER OF SEEKING AND FINDING 19

CHAPTER 3
    LEVEL 3: PRAYER OF KNOCKING AND GETTING THE DOOR OPEN 35

CHAPTER 4
    LEVEL 4: PRAYER OF VOW 47

CHAPTER 5
    LEVEL 5: PRAYER MINGLED WITH TEARS 59

CHAPTER 6
    LEVEL 6: PRAYER WITH FASTING TO OBTAIN 69

CHAPTER 7
    LEVEL 7: PRAYER WITH SACRIFICE 77

CONCLUSION **93**

NOTES **97**

PRAYERS **99**

Preface

This book is a product of my study of Hannah's prayer life in her desperation to have a child. By the inspiration and revelation of the Holy Spirit, I got to know that Hannah subconsciously took her prayer through seven levels to get her heart desire. The fact that God closed her womb for reasons best known to God, and Hannah, being unaware of God's involvement in her situation, made her desperately rely on God and solely believed that it was only God who could take her through her situation victoriously.

I believe that since God is not a respecter of persons, and what He does for one, He could do for all, Hannah's prayer, if properly understood and applied could be a prayer pattern that could solve unusual situations and predicaments that defy ordinary prayer. Thus, when it seems that your heaven is shut up, and you have done everything you know how to do in form of prayer and fasting, and your situation remains the same, instead of holding God responsible, and getting angry and frustrated, I recommend that you follow Hannah's progressive prayer, and you would also get your own Samuel (*Heard of God*).

Let us follow Hannah's prayer progression and intensity specified in the book, and classify each step she took as "Levels." Read the full account in 1 Sam 1 & 2.

Level 1: Hannah must have asked God for a child like anyone who has a desire would do. She would have prayed, "Lord, I ask that you give me a child . . ." This is the first level of prayer that I refer to as the level of *asking and receiving*. The Bible refers to it as, "Ask and it shall be given you" (Matt 7:7).

Level 2: When Hannah's situation did not change she would have asked God why her situation was different from that of her rival, Peninnah, who had sons and daughters for the same man as Hannah's husband. This is the level of *seeking and finding*. Jesus taught on this and said, "Seek and you shall find" (Matt 7:7).

Level 3: Hannah must have been aware that her situation was not ordinary, and thus, she needed to intensify her prayer. In the process, Hannah needed to "rise up after they had eaten in Shiloh, and after they had drunk . . . and was in bitterness of soul and prayed to God" (1 Sam 1: 9-10). Hanna's decision to separate herself from the crowd and family while others were eating and drinking shows her desperation and insistence which the Bible refers to as *knocking*, "Knock and it shall be opened unto you" (Matt 7:7). Hannah must have been aware at this stage that unless she persevered in prayer, whatever was shut up against her would not be open. This is what I refer to as the level of *knocking and getting the door opened*.

Level 4: Hannah made a vow that she would give her son back to God for His service (1 Sam 1:11). This prayer of vow reveals Hannah's heart. It shows that she did not want a child just for showing off her fruitfulness, but wanted a child that she would give back to God for His service. This is the kind of heart that produces the desired result in prayer.

Level 5: "Hannah wept" (1 Sam 1:7); "Hannah wept bitterly" (v. 10). It shows that Hannah shed tears that had its source from
her heart, and not just ordinary emotional tears. There are some situations that would make you shed tears in the bitterness and anguish of your soul. God is able to respond positively to such tears. See biblical examples of such tears in the book. This is the level of *prayer mingled with tears.*

Level 6: "Hannah did not eat" (1 Sam 1:7). Although not expressly stated, it is evident that Hannah must have fasted to give her prayer the necessary power, and for her voice to be heard on high. This is an important element in prayer as it is meant to give your prayer the necessary voice. This is the level I refer to as *fasting to obtain.*

Level 7: Hannah sacrificed yearly in Shiloh "a worthy potion" that her husband gave her because he loved her (1 Sam 1:6). God accepts any worthy sacrifice that is properly presented in form of our praise, reasonable service, and offering. This makes sacrifice a powerful element of prayer. Moreover, every other identified level of prayer could be complemented by sacrifice for effect, and added advantage. Hannah sacrificed again when she took Samuel to Eli in fulfillment of her vow. She presented "three bullocks, and one ephah of flour, and a bottle of wine" (v. 24). The *sacrifice* of giving up Samuel at such a tender age is a greater sacrifice for a mother who has been desperately waiting for this child for years, and who has not got any other child. This is why God responded to Hannah's sacrifice by giving her three other sons, and two daughters (1 Sam 2:21). This is the level of *sacrifice*

Have you been seeking God's face concerning an issue that seems to defy ordinary prayer? Instead of giving up, and taking it out on God, do as Hannah has done by intensifying your prayer as you take it to the next level in faith and sincerity, and you would get Hannah's kind of result. Go over the levels in greater details and for better understanding in the book; learn the principles and conditions for answered prayer in each of the levels, and be the doer of the word. Your Samuel is waiting for your celebration.

Do not give up; step up!

Introduction

The most common question people always ask me on prayer is, "What am I to do after I have prayed and my situation remains the same?" The prepared answer I used to give was "Keep on praying because the Bible says, we should pray without ceasing" (1 Thess 5:17). However, every time I came up with this biblically motivated answer, I observed that although the enquirers did accept my answer as reasonable and logical, I always perceived by their demeanor that they were far from being satisfied with my answer. They looked confused and puzzled; which showed that they wanted to know more.

I recall the last incident that happened some time ago when the enquirer, without mincing words expressed his dissatisfaction with my response and, insisted that there must be some other options to an unanswered prayer. It was there and then I knew that my stereotypical answer had finished its course. As a result, I determined to find a more convincing answer (still in the context of the scriptures), that would not only satisfy the people's curiosity but also give them the satisfaction that prayer is not a dead-end, but a dynamic and evolving relationship with God.

I have observed over the years as a minister of God that one of the most frustrating experiences in a Christian's life is praying and having no evidence of answered prayer. Such frustration could easily test the people's faith and make them lose faith and confidence in prayer, and ultimately, lose faith in God. Therefore, for a more practical and enduring answer

to the overarching question of what else to do after all prayer options have been explored, I decided to search the Bible more intently.

My search paid off because I was able to come up with what I consider as a biblically sound, and pragmatic answer, not only to the pending question, but I also discovered that prayer is an evolving and dynamic exercise that could produce the desired result if properly harnessed. My findings are harnessed to form the contents of this book.

As my research on this issue on prayer intensified, I had the opportunity to discuss the subject with my spiritual father, Bishop Sam Amao-Thomas. It is always an inspiring and exciting experience for me whenever I sit down with this knowledgeable and highly anointed man of God. On this occasion, it was more than exciting because during the course of our discussion, the Bishop intuitively showed me, more deeply, the dynamism of prayer; explaining with scriptural references that prayer is a never-ending dynamic exercise. He opined that since God answers prayer, it is our responsibility to explore different levels of prayer depending on the issue at stake and on the individual's personal relationship with God. Thus, instead of regarding prayer as a one-size-fits-all kind of thing, Bishop explained that prayer should be regarded as communing with God on various levels of relationships and needs.

Finally, I have been able to come up with what I consider as a plausible and applicable answer to the overarching question of what else to do when all prayer options have been explored and the prayer still remains unanswered. I hope this book will give you the necessary enlightenment and enhance your prayer life so much that as a Christian, you will always want to pray without being frustrated due to what you see as an unanswered prayer.

What this Book is

Many excellent Christian books have been written on the subject of prayer, with different revelations on better ways to pray for result. Some of these writings have explained in clear terms the different kinds of prayer. However, what I observe is that an average Christian is still puzzled on why his/her prayer is not answered, and is ignorant of the options open to him/her to get the desired result. While it is not possible to know all the reasons why prayers are either answered or not, I hope that the revelations found in this book would enable you to approach prayer with the right motive. That way, you may be empowered to the point that your prayer could rise to the highest level of intense fervor. In other words, this would enable you to explore the progression as depicted in the expression, *ask, seek, knock*, (Matt 7:7), which is described as "the climax depicting the rising of prayer into intense fervor"[1] What I envisage this book would do for you are the following:

- It would help you to be more organized in your prayers especially when you are desperate for an answer.
- It would help you to satisfy the condition of *praying without ceasing,* in a meaningful and effective way without making prayer repetitive or a ritual.

- It would help you overcome the hitherto attendant frustration that has been part of your prayer life as you prayed without any assurance that your prayer would be answered.

- It would generally enhance your faith in God as you focus on Him and relate with Him more intimately as a prayer-answering God.

What this Book is not

This is not just another book on prayer or about the theory of prayer, but one about the practical application of prayer. It is based on revelation and has nothing to do with the ritual of praying. Also, this book is not a panacea for answered prayer, neither is it a list of religious rites that must be fulfilled for prayers to be answered. The fact that the book identifies different levels of prayer does not mean that you must go through all the levels before your prayer could be answered, or go straight to explore the higher levels because of the grievousness of your situation. God's prerogative to answer any kind of prayer any how He wants, and at any time He decides, is undisputable, and is therefore, given its prominent place in the contents of this book. In fact, God could decide to answer someone who has not prayed the conventional way as He knows every person's thoughts and meditation. The Psalmist says, *"Let the words of my mouth and the meditation of my heart be acceptable in your sight, O Lord my strength and my redeemer" (Ps 19:11).*

It is also evident that God answers prayers at the time appropriate to Him. The Bible says, *"And it will be, before they call I will answer; and while they are still speaking, I will hear" (Isa 65:24).* Generally, God cannot be put in a strait jacket when it comes to His faithfulness in answering prayers. The Bible says, *"Now to Him who is able to do exceeding abundantly above all that we **ask** or **think**, according to the power that works in us (Eph 3:20, emphasis added).*

In my attempt to make this book as practical and pragmatic as possible, I highlight some biblical principles involved in some prayers that received God's blessings in the Bible, coupled with some personal examples and applications. I expect that these references would enhance your faith, and make you have greater confidence in appreciating God's faithfulness.

Also, since principles are for general applications, I hope that you would be able to apply these principles into your personal life situations. The fact that principles do not change, makes the outcome of such applied principles predictable. The Bible says, *For whatever things were written before were written for our learning, that we through the patience and comfort of the Scriptures might have hope. (Rom 15:4),* The revelation in this book and its biblical application is to make you have hope that what God did for one, He could do for all. For instance, making Hannah a reference point is to enable you to understand what Hannah did differently that made her situation change positively. I hope and pray that as you read this book, and apply the principles highlighted therein to your situations, those situation would also change for better.

More importantly, as you read through the pages of this book, I hope that you would be inspired to see yourself in the book, and your prayer life would not be the same again. Just as God has revealed to me the answer to the age long question on prayer, I hope that you would also find the solution to that pending situation of your life, no matter how long you've sought for the solution. Again, I hope that your prayer life would be greatly enhanced.

CHAPTER 1

Level 1: Prayer of Asking and Receiving

> *Ask and it will be given to you;* seek and you will find; knock and the door will be opened to you. *⁸ For everyone who asks receives;* the one who seeks finds; and to the one who knocks, the door will be opened (Matt 7:7-8, emphasis added)

The first level of prayer that is common to everyone who prays is the level of Asking. This is the meeting point of prayers as everyone who prays normally has some desires to commit to God. As you commit your desires to God, you are engaging in the prayer of Asking, with the expectation of receiving. In Greek, to ask in the context of prayer is *aiteo* meaning, "to beg, call for, crave, desire, and require" (Strong's Gk, 154).

The assurance and confidence we have in prayer is that God is a gracious God, who would not deny His children the things they deserve. Jesus affirms this assertion in one of His teachings on prayer, "If you, then, though you are evil, know how to give good gifts to your children, how much more will your Father in heaven give good gifts to those who ask him!" (Matt 7:11).

The implication of this declaration is that it is the responsibility of the individual to ask, with the assurance that when the asking is done, the receiving will take place. Some people question the need to ask an all-knowing and merciful God who is expected to know their needs, and give them whatever they need without asking Him. May be you are also struggling with this thought, and as a result, your prayer life is negatively affected. I want you to know that although God is all-knowing, He would not want to interfere with your freedom of choice. Thus, God would not impose on you anything that you do not request from Him. In other words, it is when you ask that you receive. The scripture is clear on this.

People's demands are not the same. As a result, the prayer of Asking varies from person to person, but the approach is always the same. For instance, someone's need might be physical; like food, clothing, and shelter, while another person's need might be healing of the body; and yet another's need might be victory over his/her enemies. These are all needs, which could be asked for with the expectation that God would grant them to those who ask in faith. In what follows, we will look at some biblical examples of prayer of asking.

Let us consider the story of Solomon. The Bible says, *"At Gibeon the LORD appeared to Solomon in a dream by night; and God said, "**Ask**! What shall I give you?" (1 Kings 3:5, emphasis) added).* You would observe in this passage that God did not take what Solomon needed for granted, but gave him the opportunity to express his wish by asking. This is because God wanted Solomon to take responsibility for his demands, without God imposing anything on him. This is a confirmation that God responds to demands that are presented in prayer. One thing that you would observe from Solomon's request is its *specificity*.

Listen to Solomon's specific demand, "Therefore give to Your servant an understanding heart to judge Your people, that I may discern between good and evil. For who is able to judge this great people of Yours?" (v. 9). This request for an understanding heart is specific as a requirement for making righteous judgment, and God was satisfied that Solomon did not ask for selfish and material things which characterize most people's requests. Listen to God's response,

> *Because you have asked this thing, and have not asked long life for yourself, nor have asked riches for yourself, nor have asked the life of your enemies, but have asked for yourself understanding to discern justice, ^{12} behold, I have done **according to your words;** see, I have given you a wise and understanding heart, so that there has not been anyone like you before you, nor shall any like you arise after you (vv. 11-13, emphasis added).*

God's response is according to Solomon's words. This is why it is imperative to ask with clarity and specificity because God would always want to respond according to the person's demand.

Another example is Hannah. Hannah was barren, and wanted a child. In her request, she was specific as she asked for *"a man child" (1 Sam 1:11, KJV)*. She did not assume that God should know what kind of a child she needed, but specified a male child. Not just that, Hannah was so clear in her request that she even told God the kind of male child she wanted, and what type of destiny she envisaged for the child. She vowed, *"I will give him to the LORD all the days of his life, and no razor shall come upon his head" (v. 11)*. This is one of the reasons why God remembered Hannah and granted her request.

Let me show you someone who did not ask and how frustrated he was. He is the unnamed brother of the Prodigal Son (Lk 15:11-32). According to the story, when the brother of the Prodigal Son was some distance away from home on his return from the day's work, he asked for the reason for the celebration and merriment that the father had planned for his brother who "was dead, and is alive again; was lost and is found" (v. 32). He became dejected and frustrated to learn that the father was celebrating the return of his brother who, according to him, had wasted the father's resources in riotous living. He complained to his father, *"Lo, these many years I have been serving you; I never transgressed your commandment at any time;* **and yet you never gave me a young goat, that I might make merry with my friends"** *(v. 29, emphasis added)*. He expected the father to give due to his loyalty, even when he did not ask. Listen to the father's response. "Son, you are always with me, and all that I have is yours" (v. 31). In other words, it is true that you have always been with me, and as a heir of the estate, all things belong to you, but you do not celebrate and merry because you do not ask. It is the same with you as a child of the most high God. You are a joint heir with Jesus, and all things belong to you. However, you cannot take God's blessings for granted, but must ask so that you could receive, and be merry.

The fact that specificity is a condition for answered prayer shows that there are some other conditions that must be satisfied for your demands to be granted. God's blessings come with some conditions, and here are some of the conditions for asking and receiving.

Conditions for Asking and Receiving

1. You must ask in faith.
It is not just enough to ask God for things without backing your request up with faith. Jesus taught about this subject in Mark 11:23-24. The disciples wondered how a tree, which has no ability to comprehend, could respond to Jesus' command when He uttered these words, *"Let no one eat fruit from you ever again" (Mk 11:14).* In response, Jesus taught that the disciples could do the same if they had faith in God, or have God's kind of faith. He taught, *"Therefore I say to you, whatever things you ask when you pray, believe that you receive them, and you will have them" (v. 24),* which means that you must believe that your prayer is answered as you pray, and not necessarily when the situation looks favorable. Jesus emphasized that it is when you believe that you would see the manifestation of your request, and not the other way round. This is why the Bible says, *"But without faith it is impossible to please Him" (Heb 11:6).* In other words, God responds to faith rather than to needs, because God would not

grant any need not supported by faith. The opposite of faith is doubt and unbelief. Any time you doubt in your prayer, the prayer becomes ineffective. For example, if you are asking God for a job, and you have done all the necessary things including filling out applications, and following up with calls or visits to the places you've applied to, if in the course of your prayer you doubt, because you think that the high unemployment rate reported in the news could affect your chances of getting the job, then you have just nullified your chances of getting that job. The Bible collaborates this point when Apostle James wrote, *"For let not that man suppose that he will receive anything from the Lord; he is a double-minded man, unstable in all his ways" (Jms 1:7-8).* Therefore, even when circumstances appear unfavorable in the natural, you should still believe because faith operates in the unseen realm, which makes the physical manifestation possible.

2. Praying according to God's Will

In prayer, your will or desire must correspond with God's will. You may wonder why God's will is important. It is because God is committed to His Word to fulfill it (Jer 1:12). The Bible says, *"For You have magnified Your word above all Your name" (Ps 138:12).* God is so righteous that He will never do anything to deny Himself, or His Word. Therefore, if there is anything that should serve as your anchor in prayer, it is what God has said He would do in His Word. This is His will! He assures, *"So shall My word be that goes forth from My mouth; It shall not return to Me void, But it shall accomplish what I please, And it shall prosper in the thing for which I sent it" (Isa 55:11).* Thus, God is obligated to do whatever He has said He would do. One of the greatest secrets in prayer is that as you pray God's word, He hears Himself; and because He cannot deny Himself, He cannot deny your prayer. *"Does he speak and then not act? Does he promise and not fulfill?" (Num 23:19, NIV).*

Therefore, for you to pray an effective prayer that lines up with God's will, you should search through the Bible to bring out the particular Word that pertains to your situation. When you find God's will as expressed in His Word, you have got an essential ingredient for your prayer as God's faithfulness would not make Him to deny what He has said. Jesus taught the same principle when He said, *"If you abide in Me, and My words abide in you, you will ask what you desire, and it shall be done for you" (Jn 15:7).* As you abide in Christ as a believer, and His word abides in you--committing it to heart and believing it--using the same words in your prayer gives the assurance that it will be done to you.

This means that in prayer it is not your will that is important, it is God's will. The late preacher, Myles Monroe, once said, "Prayer is not emphasizing your will to make it come to pass. Rather, prayer is approaching God in order to ask Him to accomplish His will in the earth."[2]

A Biblical example of praying God's will is recorded in Acts 4:13-31. Following the religious people's threat of imprisonment and death to the disciples for preaching at Jerusalem, the disciples decided to pray God's will so that God would give them the boldness with which they would continue to preach the gospel in spite of the threat to their lives. Listen to their prayer as recorded in Acts 4:24-30,

> *So when they heard that, they raised their voice to God with one accord and said: "Lord, You are God,*

who made heaven and earth and the sea, and all that is in them, who by the mouth of Your servant David have said:

*'Why did the nations rage,
And the people plot vain things?
The kings of the earth took their stand, And the rulers were gathered together against the* LORD *and against His Christ.'*

"For truly against Your holy Servant Jesus, whom You anointed, both Herod and Pontius Pilate, with the Gentiles and the people of Israel, were gathered together [28] *to do whatever Your hand and Your purpose determined before to be done.* [29] *Now, Lord, look on their threats, and grant to Your servants that with all boldness they may speak Your word,* [30] *by stretching out Your hand to heal, and that signs and wonders may be done through the name of Your holy Servant Jesus" (Acts 4:24-30).*

You could see how the disciples expressed God's will as found in Ps 2:1-2. (See vv. 25 and 26 of the prayer). They did this because this particular scripture is relevant to their situation. God's response to their prayer was a confirmation that their prayer got God's attention. The Bible says, *"And when they had prayed, the place where they were assembled together was shaken; and they were all filled with the Holy Spirit, and they spoke the word of God with boldness" (v. 31).*

Following the filling of the Holy Spirit, they had the boldness with which they could preach the gospel, meaning that their prayer was answered. The Bible records, *"The disciples went out, preaching the gospel with boldness" (v. 35).* What this boils down to is the indispensability of the Word of God in praying God's will. It shows that every Christian needs the Word for a victorious Christian life. The Word is an essential ingredient for prayer without which prayer is meaningless. I have observed that those who don't have the time for the Word are those who usually pay "prayer warriors" to help them pray. The problem is that such a prayer could not be effective because money would not buy any answer from the Throne of Grace. There is nothing intrinsically wrong in praying with prayer partners, but when prayer is "contracted out" it is not likely to be the kind of prayer that could change situations, let alone move mountains.

3. You must avoid sin

When there is sin in your life, God will not hear you. The Bible makes it clear that:

> *"If I regard iniquity in my heart, The Lord will not hear" (Ps 66:18).*
>
> *"But your iniquities have separated you from your God; And your sins have hidden His face from you, So that He will not hear" (Isa 59:2).*
>
> *"And whatever we ask we receive from Him, because we keep His commandments and do those things that are pleasing in His sight" (1 Jn 3:22).*

You should confess and repent of your sins, not as a formality, but genuinely because repentance means that you would not go back to those sins that had hitherto separated you from God. Anyone who is separated from God by sin has no hope of getting God's attention, and cannot have his prayer answered.

4. You must not pray in fear
When you pray in fear, it shows that your faith is not involved; and anything a person does without faith cannot please God (Heb 11:6). Fear will hinder you from having the necessary freedom and confidence needed to approach God in prayer. Listen to what the Bible says:

> *"Therefore, brethren, having boldness to enter the Holiest by the blood of Jesus" (Heb 10:19).*
>
> *"For God has not given us a spirit of fear, but of power and of love and of a sound mind" (2 Tim 1:7).*

5. You must not pray with the wrong motive
The motive behind your prayer is very important because it determines if God would answer your prayer or not. Although your motive may be hidden from man, it cannot be hidden from God because God knows the purpose and intent of every heart. The Bible says, *"You ask and do not receive, because you ask amiss, that you may spend it on your pleasures" (Jms 4:3).* This is why selfish prayers have no place with God.

6. You must not pray with an unforgiving heart
It is necessary for you to search your heart to determine if there is anyone or people you have not forgiven for the wrong they had done against you. Such an unforgiving spirit will certainly hinder your prayer. No matter how hurtful the offence might be, God still holds you responsible to forgive

for the fact that God Himself has forgiven you of all your sins. Jesus taught this important lesson in His prayer, "And forgive us our debts, As we forgive our debtors" (Matt 6:12).

In another teaching on prayer, Jesus says,

> *And whenever you stand praying, if you have anything against anyone, forgive him, that your Father in heaven may also forgive you your trespasses. [26] But if you do not forgive, neither will your Father in heaven forgive your trespasses (Mk 11:25-26).*

In one of Paul's teachings, he wrote, *"Let all bitterness, wrath, anger, clamor, and evil speaking be put away from you, with all malice. And be kind to one another, tenderhearted, forgiving one another, even as God in Christ forgave you" (Eph 4:31-32).*

These are some of the conditions for answered prayer, and they are meant to inspire you to live right and guide you against anything that could hinder your prayer. They are not like rituals to be followed, but conditions to be fulfilled, and the fulfillment comes easily as you grow in faith and get more intimate with God in your relationship with Him.

CHAPTER 2

Level 2: Prayer of Seeking and Finding

> *Ask, and it will be given to you;* ***seek, and you will find****; knock, and it will be opened to you. ⁸ For everyone who asks receives, and* ***he who seeks finds****, and to him who knocks it will be opened (Matt 7:7-8, emphasis added).*

There are times you pray and do not have the expected response from God. Instead of your situation improving, there seems to be either no change, or the situation gets worse. You become confused and agitated, and desperately want to know why God, who promised to give good things to those who ask Him, is not responding to your prayer. Let me draw a biblical parallel of such a situation in the story of the Syrophoenician woman who sought Jesus for the healing of her demon-possessed daughter (Matt 15:22-28). According to the account, the woman cried out for help, *"Have mercy on me, O Lord, Son of David! My daughter is severely demon-*

possessed." (v. 22). People's call for mercy always gets Jesus' attention, like the call of Bartmeaus. He cried out, *"Jesus, son of David, have mercy on me!" (Mk 10:47)*. In Bartmeaus' case, Jesus responded as He "stood still," and healed him (v. 49). But in the case of the Syrophoenician woman the Bible say, *"But He answered her not a word" (v. 23)*.

There are times we make our request to God, and He does not seem to respond. In such a situation, it is tempting to question God's faithfulness and justice. You are also likely to doubt your faith or feel guilty for a perceived sin. However, an important lesson to learn from the Syrophoenician woman is her insistence to know why Jesus refused to respond to her. She did not give up like some of us would do whenever it seems we are not receiving the expected response to our prayer. The Bible says, "Then she came and worshiped Him, saying, "Lord, help me!" (v. 25). It was at this point that Jesus showed her why He did not respond to her. He explained, *"It is not good to take the children's bread and throw it to the little dogs." (v. 26)*.

There is a critical point in this scenario. Imagine if the Syrophoenician woman did not enquire to know why Jesus decided not to answer her; there was no way she would have known, and sadly, she would have missed her miracle. But it was in her determination to get an answer that she knew why Jesus did not respond to her request. Jesus' explanation must have activated the woman's faith, which made her respond, *"Yes, Lord, yet even the little dogs eat the crumbs which fall from their masters' table." (v. 27)*. Jesus saw in her response an evidence of "great faith" which qualified her for Jesus' compassion and the instant healing of her daughter.

What does it mean to seek?

What I want to point out in this incident is the missing link in some of our prayers, which is the element of seeking. When some people do not receive an immediate answer to their prayers, they become discouraged, frustrated, and disappointed. But instead of pressing further by seeking to know why God does not respond to them, they easily take offence and shut down on God. In the process, they give up all their spiritual activities like Bible reading and taking part in church activities. Such people usually act on impulse, not knowing that their negative reaction can never be the answer to their problem. If anything at all, it could compound their problems the more.

What I would recommend in such a situation is to seek God for the reason for His silence. As you seek, you would get to know why your prayer is not answered, and what you have to do to get God's attention. It is important to know that the word *seek* means to **actively** look for something. It does not mean to look casually or to see unintentionally. It implies activeness and intentionality. Thus, the believer does not keep quiet after thinking he or she has not received what is being asked for, but he/she seeks to know why and what to do to get the desired result.

Another element in the prayer of seeking is seeking God's guidance and direction, especially in our decision making process. You seek God for the direction to take in respect of a decision you are contemplating on. Seeking God for direction is Scriptural because God says, "I will instruct you and teach you in the way you should go; I will guide you with My eye" (Ps 32:8). This is a very important aspect of prayer, which many are not aware of, and which makes them get easily frustrated. Therefore, instead of allowing frustration to take a better part of your prayer life due to what you consider as unanswered prayer, I suggest you take a step further of seeking to know why God has not responded, and what next you have to do.

There are times we pray, and God responds, but because His response falls short of our expectation, it seems to us as if He has not responded. The fact of the matter is that God's response could be in different forms. It could be "I have heard you, but wait." This kind of response does not resonate with us easily because we always want instant manifestation of God's response. God's response could be outright "no." Although you do not expect such a response, you should aspire to know why God gives such a response. You could do this by seeking Him in prayer. The intention is not to question God, but to enquire in humility. When you seek, you will find! Incidentally, since God has the prerogative of answering prayers the best way reasonable to Him, what you regard as delay or denial might turn out to be the best response in your particular circumstance. In any case, there is no way you could know what is in God's mind, except you seek in prayer.

Another aspect of seeking is to enquire in order to know what is yet to be revealed. It is interesting to note that the word *seek* is the same in the Hebrew language as *bagash* (Strong's, Hebrew 1245), which is a prime root word for the phrase, *search out*, especially in prayer. By implication, bagash means, "to ask, beg, beseech, desire, and enquire" (*enquire* is a word commonly used in the Old Testament). God is known as the giver of good things to those who ask Him (Matt 7:11), but when you don't have the good things after asking, it is logical to find out the missing link. Since God's thoughts are not the same as our thoughts, and His ways are different from our ways (Isa 55:10), you must find a common ground by which God's thoughts and ways would make sense to you. This is only possible when you seek in prayer.

I recall an incident in which I was interceding for someone who had health issues for about two weeks, without any change in his condition, but instead, the person's condition got worse. This gave me the determination to find out what I needed to know about the situation that I had not known, or what I, or the person, needed to do to facilitate a change in his situation. After seeking God in prayer, God revealed to me what the problem was, including the solution to the problem. As I did what God revealed to me, the situation of the sick person started getting better, and he was eventually healed of his sickness. If I did not venture to seek God, there was no way I could have known the solution to the situation. Thus, we are sometimes just one prayer away from the solution to our problems, and that prayer is the prayer of seeking.

I have discovered why this aspect of prayer remains unexplored by some people. This is due to the fact that some people regard prayer as a monologue--that is a one-way communication with God. On the contrary, prayer is be a dialogue, or conversation. When you regard prayer as a dialogue, you would not do all the talking, but would give God the chance to also talk back to you. It is important for God's children to know that God also wants to speak to us, but we hinder Him by not giving Him the chance as we do all the talking. More importantly, God wants to show you His secret that you would never know unless He reveals them to you. The Bible says, *"The secret things belong to the LORD our God, but those things which are revealed belong to us and to our children forever, that we may do all the words of this law" (Deut 29:29).* Until secret things are revealed to you, they remain concealed.

This is why it is your responsibility to pray for the secrets things to be revealed. The Bible says, *"It is the glory of God to conceal a matter, But the glory of kings is to search out a matter" (Prov 25:2).* As a believer, you have been made a king and priest unto the Lord (Rev 5:10). Therefore, whatever secret is concealed must be searched out because that is where your honor is. God says, *"Call to Me, and I will answer you, and show you great and mighty things, which you do not know" (Jer 33:3).* This is an assurance that God is interested in responding to our desire to know secrets things, as we call unto Him. Let us look at some biblical examples of how some people sought God in their prayers and got His response.

Biblical Examples

One of David's secrets is his intimate relationship with God for which God refers to him as *"a man after my heart" (1 Sam 13:14).* David's relationship with God was so intimate that He used to have seven worship sessions with God daily. David said, *"Seven times a day I praise You, Because of Your righteous judgments" (Ps 119:164).* His intimate relationship gave David the confidence to approach God for guidance in almost every situation he found himself. Thus, David is an example of a seeker in prayer. Let us look into some of the ways David sought God in prayer.

As a man of war, David did not take his skills and ability in battle for granted. Although he has a long testimony of victories in his favor, including the defeat of Goliath, yet, he was always seeking God's timing and support in the battles confronting him. For instance, in the battle with the Philistines who were apparently the aggressors, David took time to seek God's guidance, and the possible warfare strategy he could adopt. He enquired, *"Shall I go up against the Philistines? Will You deliver them into my hand?" And the LORD said to David, "Go up, for I will doubtless deliver the Philistines into your hand" (2 Sam 5:19)*. This statement became David's motivation, believing that God would do exactly as He has said. What do you think would be the outcome of a battle that God says He has doubtlessly fought and won? As many times as the Philistines came up to the Israelites in battle, David did seek God's guidance and intervention without assuming that if he could defeat them once, he would be able to do it again. Following God's instructions, David was always victorious (see 2 Sam 21:1; 22:25).

In one of his Psalms, David wrote of his experience in seeking God for guidance, *"I sought the LORD, and He heard me, And delivered me from all my fears. ⁵ They looked to Him and were radiant, And their faces were not ashamed" (Ps 34:4-5)*. If you have not been seeking God in your prayers, a fact that has led to your frustration and doubt, I advise that you follow David's example by taking time to seek God for the solution to your problems. Just as David celebrated victories after victories, you too would come out with songs of victory.

Prayer of seeking is not limited to issues that are yet to be answered, they could also be on issues that are answered, but still need some clarification or affirmation. There is a good example to this fact in the story of Rebecca, Isaac's wife. Rebecca had an unusual kind of pregnancy because *"the children struggled together within her" (Gen 25:22),* and needed to know why the babies were behaving in this unusual manner. Rachael enquired, *"If all is well, why am I like this?"* In response, God said, *"Two nations are in your womb, Two peoples shall be separated from your body; One people shall be stronger than the other, And the older shall serve the younger"(v. 23).* There was no way Rebecca would have known the reason for the peculiar behavior of these unborn babies without deliberately inquiring. In her enquiry, she even got more than she asked for; she got to know the destiny of the babies.

May be you are contemplating on relocating, for example, and do not know where to relocate to, or you have been seeking God for a future spouse, and seems there is no response after you have prayed. I want to suggest that you enquire why your request seems unanswered. You would be surprised by God's response, as He might show you secrets concerning your situation that you would never have known, and which could be the pointer to the answer to your prayer.

I heard the story of how God revealed Himself to a businessman who wanted to know why his business was on the down turn. As the businessman was seeking God for the solution to his dwindling business, the Holy Spirit revealed to him the cause of his problem. It was revealed that the businessman was not faithful with his tithes, which made the devourer to enter his business. The business man repented, and determined to start paying his tithes. As he kept paying his tithes, the story has a happy ending because the man's business started prospering, and after some months, the man testified to God's faithfulness. If the businessman did not seek to know the reason for his failing business, there was no way he would have known the solution. Therefore, instead of asking for the same thing over and over in your prayer for which there is no change, I suggest that you seek God to know why the situation remains the same, and you would be surprised what the Lord would reveal to you.

Identifying the difference between asking and seeking

Perhaps you are still confused in differentiating between the prayers of asking and seeking, I want to make some clarification by applying the Word of God to show the difference.

> *For I know the plans and thoughts that I have for you," says the* LORD, *"plans for peace and well-being and not for disaster to give you a future and a hope. Then you will call on Me and you will come and* **pray** *to Me, and I will hear [your voice] and I will listen to you. Then [with a deep longing] you will* **seek** *Me and require Me [as a vital necessity] and [you will] find Me when you search for Me with all your heart (Jer 29:11-13, AMP, emphasis added).*

In this passage, God urges the people to pray and seek Him. This represents two different kinds of actions: praying and seeking. In other words, the people should pray to ask for the fulfillment of God's plan for them. They should also seek

God with a deep longing and as a vital necessity, presumably if they pray and it seems to them that God does not hear them, they would need to seek to know the reason for God's silence.

Many centuries after God had given the children of Israel this injunction, they found themselves in captivity in Babylon, and wanted to know if God had forgotten them. Daniel understood by Jeremiah's prophecy that *"he would accomplish seventy years in the desolations of Jerusalem" (Daniel 9:2)*. So, Daniel decided to seek God for the future of Israel as he wanted to know God's plan for the people. Thus, Daniel enquired in prayer, saying: *"Then I set my face toward the Lord God to make request by prayer and supplications, with fasting, sackcloth, and ashes. ⁴ And I prayed to the LORD my God, and made confession . . . " (Daniel 9:3-4)*.

It is clear in this passage that Daniel prayed for the forgiveness of the sins of the nation, and also sought to know why they were not restored to their land after the completion of the seventy years of captivity. In response, God showed him the vision of *Seventy Weeks* (Dan 9: 24-27). Considering Daniel's approach in this prayer, it shows that one should not take God's promise for granted. Every one of God's promises must be claimed and possessed by faith for it to be fulfilled. Even though God told the children of Israel that His thought towards them were for good and not for evil, and to give them hope and an expected end, they were still needed to follow up by seeking God with all their heart (Jer 29: 11-14). Therefore, whenever it seems that things are not going well for you as you claim God's promises, you should seek God to know what you need to do to accomplish the promise. Seeking is for those who aspire to find!

Conditions for Seeking in Prayer

> *If My people who are called by My name will humble themselves, and pray and seek My face, and turn from their wicked ways, then I will hear from heaven, and will forgive their sin and heal their land (2 Chr 2:14).*

This Scripture shows that there are conditions for seeking God in prayer. Humility and repentance are two conditions identified in this Scripture. Let us consider in detail, the conditions for prayer of seeking.

1. You must seek in humility.
"If my people . . . will humble themselves . . . " (v. 14). Why is humility an essential condition for seeking God? It is because the secret of God is revealed to the humble. The Bible says, *"The secret of the LORD is with those who fear Him, And He will show them His covenant" (Ps 25:14)*. Also by God's standard, it is only the humble that are qualified for promotion.

> *Yes, all of you be submissive to one another, and be clothed with humility, for "God resists the proud, But gives grace to the humble" Therefore humble yourselves under the mighty hand of God, that He may exalt you in due time, (1 Pet 5:5-6).*

The opposite of humility is pride, which means that the proud has no access to God's secrets because God resists them. God regards the proud as those who disregard His commandments and by implication, disregard Him. Such people have fallen out of God's favor, and therefore, have no access to God's secrets.

2. You must seek in prayer.

Although God says you should seek Him, you should not lose sight of prayer as the platform for seeking God. Thus, seeking God should not be misunderstood to mean that you should use prayer as a medium for fortune telling or clairvoyance. Rather, you are expected to seek when you have the need to enquire about specific issues pertaining to your desire. The platform for seeking must always be that of prayer and everything you do in seeking must be done reverently.

3. You must live righteously.

It is important to know that secret things do not belong to everyone. Secret things belong only to the righteous--those who are in right standing with God. As every believer has been made the righteousness of God through Jesus Christ, we must aspire to live righteously (2 Cor 5:21). When you are in right standing with God, you are qualified for His secrets. The Bible says, *"For the perverse person is an abomination to the LORD, But His secret counsel is with the upright" (Prov 3:32).* Even when you are not faithful, God is always faithful. This is why you should believe Him when He says, *"No good thing will He withhold from those who walk uprightly" (Ps 84:11).*

4. You must be identified as God's child.

Let us go back to the passage referenced earlier: *"If my people who are called by my name . . ." (2 Chro 7:14).* This presupposes identification with God. As a believer, you are a new creature, born again into the new life in Christ. As a result of this status, every born again Christian is regarded as a child of God, and is therefore, qualified to approach God as his/her Father. Although He is God of both believers and unbelievers, and causes it to rain on them both without any discrimination, yet, God has special preference for those who are identifiable with Him through the redemptive blood of Jesus. The Bible says, *"But as many as received Him, to them He gave the right to become children of God, to those who believe in His name" Jn 1:12).*

Thus, if you have not confessed Jesus as your Lord and Savior, or you are in doubt of your standing with God, I advise that you take the bold step to be in right standing with God by confessing Christ as your Lord and Savior. You may be wondering why it is so simple to be saved, and become a child of God. There is no doubt that God does not put any burden on people. This would explain why He made His only begotten Son Jesus to pay the price you would have paid for your sins, which is death (Rom 3:25). All it takes is for you to identify with what Jesus did on the cross, and you are considered saved (Rom 10:9-10).

5. You must seek God wholeheartedly

"And you will seek Me and find Me, when you search for Me with all your heart" (Jer 29:13). What does it mean to search for God with all your heart? First, it means absolute dedication. When praying to seek, you must focus on God. When you are not focused, it means that your mind is divided and according to the Word of God, a divided mind cannot receive anything from God (Jms 1:8). Another evidence of focus is Trust. Thus, you seek God when you have no other alternative plan. For instance, if you have a plan in your mind

that "If I don't get what I want from God, I will go and see my psychic," you should not expect to get anything from God. Anyone who has such a mind is not wholehearted with God, and cannot receive God's secret.

Lastly, this is not the kind of prayer that you pray when you are engrossed in your daily busyness, or when you are anxious. You must maintain a tranquil environment because it is in such an environment that you can hear God clearly. Thus, it is difficult to be in tune with God, and be wholehearted with Him in a busy, and noisy environment that characterize our lives today. I therefore, recommend that as you seek God, you must separate yourself for concentration and focus.

6. You must be a true worshipper of God

One indisputable way God reveals Himself to people is in worship. When you are a true worshipper, you have access to the throne of grace, and hence, to God's secrets. The Bible says, "God is Spirit, and those who worship Him must worship in spirit and truth" (Jn 4:24). You truly worship God in the spirit and not in your body. In this respect, the condition of your heart must reflect true worship. The Bible says, *"For the Father is seeking such to worship Him" (v. 23).* Seek God in spirit and in truth, and you will be in agreement with Him for His secrets and revelations.

In the prayer of seeking, the role of the Holy Spirit is profound as He helps you to pray better than you could by your own efforts and understanding. What is more, the Holy Spirit is the revealer of God's secrets, for He knows God's mind (Jn 16:23). Therefore, you must take the Holy spirit as your prayer companion; and whatever appears hidden would be revealed by Him. It is when you seek and find that your prayer is answered.

However, it is possible to seek with all your heart, and fulfill all the conditions mentioned above, and yet not find an answer to your situation. Hannah was in such a predicament that she must have prayed all kinds of prayer, and yet her situation remained the same. More so, when she did not know that it was God who had closed her womb (1 Sam 1:6). However, Hannah did not give up, but continued to pray, and in the process, intuitively progressed to what I regard as *knocking* in prayer, which is the focus of the next chapter.

CHAPTER 3

Level 3: Prayer of Knocking and Getting the Door Open

> Ask, and it will be given to you; seek, and you will find; **knock, and it will be opened to you.** [8] For everyone who asks receives, and he who seeks finds, **and to him who knocks it will be opened** (Matt 7:7-8, emphasis added)

The third level of prayer is the level of knocking, which is better known as the prayer of insistence and persistence. Let us consider the Parable of the persistent widow for a better understanding of this kind of prayer:

> *Then He spoke a parable to them, that men always ought to pray and not lose heart, saying: "There was in a certain city a judge who did not fear God nor regard man. Now there was a widow in that city; and she came to him, saying, 'Get justice for me from my adversary.' And he would not for a while; but afterward he said within himself, 'Though*

I do not fear God nor regard man, yet because this widow troubles me I will avenge her, lest by her continual coming she weary me.' Then the Lord said, "Hear what the unjust judge said. And shall God not avenge His own elect who cry out day and night to Him, though He bears long with them? I tell you that He will avenge them speedily. Nevertheless, when the Son of Man comes, will He really find faith on the earth?"(Lk 18:1-8).

This parable shows a desperate widow who wanted justice by all means, and would not want to take 'no' for an answer, even though she was aware that the judge was not a compassionate person, yet he was forced to respond to the widow's plea due to her persistent pressure. This was why the judge said within himself, *"Though I do not fear God nor regard man, yet because this widow troubles me I will avenge her, lest by her continual coming she weary me."* Jesus concludes the parable by asking rhetorically, *"And shall God not avenge His own elect who cry out day and night to Him, though He bears long with them? I tell you that He will avenge them speedily" (Lk 18:4-8).*

This is a confirmation that our good and compassionate God will always respond to the plea of those who seek Him persistently and consistently. This Scripture opens with the injunction that *"men always ought to pray and not lose heart" (v. 1)*. How you could be expectedly persistent in prayer without wearing yourself out will be explained in this section.

For proper understanding of the concept of knocking, it is necessary to consider the imagery of knocking from the eastern Mediterranean cultural background. In the Eastern culture, it is normal for someone to knock at his/her neighbor's door at any time of the day or night to ask for something that he/she needs for daily use, like salt, pepper, vegetable, or food. No matter the time, the neighbor is obligated to respond to the neighbor's request as he/she knocks.

In their book, *Aramaic Light on the Gospels of Mark and Luke,* Rocco Errico and George Lamsa identify different kinds of knocking in the Eastern culture.[3] In that culture, a host is able to identify the person knocking by the kind of sound produced at the door. For instance, a traveler knocks with his cane or stone; and the host responds by opening the door to give the traveler food, or shelter or whatever assistance he or she might need. The people understand that a beggar does not knock the door directly, but taps the floor near the door with his/her cane. The host responds by opening the door to give the beggar food or water.

In another parable of similar significance, a friend goes to another friend's house to knock at his door at midnight because he needs bread to set before a traveler who has just arrived from a journey (Lk 11:5-8). A sign of intimate friendship in the Eastern culture is hospitability which is usually demonstrated by sharing food with travelers no matter the time of the day or night the traveler arrives. In this parable, the host goes to knock at a friend's door at midnight when the family has gone to bed. Although the owner of the house would not want to open the door because it was midnight and his family was already in bed, the Bible says that he would open the door to attend to his friend's request because of the friend's *importunity (KJV); boldness (NIV);* or *shameless persistence and insistence (AMP)*; or *standing your ground, knocking and waking all the neighbors (MSG)*. What is emphasized here is the friend's insistence and persistence to get what he wants from the owner of the house, to satisfy the traveler.

There are times you are faced with this kind of situation in which you are desperate and determined to get God's attention concerning your situation. You are determined for a change in that situation you've been dealing with for some time. In other words, you are at the point at which you need a breakthrough or the situation breaks you into pieces. As a result, in your desperation, you keep knocking at heaven's door for God's grace and mercy. This is what is usually referred to as "divine heavenly disturbance." This is not the time for false humility or undue timidity. It is time to impress on the Throne of Grace and let the Father know that "Dad, I am at Your mercy. Save me or I perish!" Let us consider some cases from the bible.

Biblical Examples

Hannah exemplifies a classical case of a desperate woman. She showed her desperation to have a child in her prayer. On the occasion of the family's visit to Shiloh to worship, the Bible says that she decided to stay back alone in the temple to pray a heart-felt prayer, when other worshippers and members of her family were feasting outside the temple. Eli, the High Priest, observed Hannah as she prayed, and her demeanor of persistence and desperation appeared to Eli as someone who was drunk. The Bible says, *"Only her lips moved, but her voice was not heard" (v. 13).* Hannah, however, explained her situation to Eli as that of a woman pouring out her soul before the Lord. Her prayer eventually evoked Eli's blessing as he declared with prophetic authority that, *"Go in peace, and the God of Israel grant your petition which you have asked of Him" (v. 17).*

Another example is Jacob who was in a desperate situation on his return journey from Laban, his uncle, where he had sojourned for about twenty years after he stole Esau's birthright. Jacob was really blessed while he was with Laban, and returned with a large family and great possession of livestock, with men and maidservants. However, since he had no means of communicating with Esau for the years of their separation, he had no idea how Esau would react to him, for he feared Esau's revenge. Thus, Jacob decided to appease Esau so that he would not retaliate by attacking him and thereby destroy his family and livestock. After making the plan to appease Esau with some gifts, Jacob was still not sure of Esau's reaction. Thus, he decided to seek God's intervention in the matter. His plea was, *"Deliver me, I pray, from the hand of my brother, from the hand of Esau; for I fear him, lest he come and attack me and the mother with the children" (Gen 32:11).* Read the full story in Gen 32.

Jacob did not want to pray this prayer in a hurry or squeeze some minutes of prayer out of his busy schedule, with his family and livestock lurking around him. Rather, he planned to be left alone like Hannah, while he allowed others to go ahead of him. As Jacob travailed in prayer, the Bible described his encounter as wrestling with God (v. 24). In fact, the sub-title of that particular passage in NIV is, *Jacob wrestles with God.* At the break of the day when the man with whom Jacob was wrestling requested to leave, Jacob showed his desperation as he held on to him, insisting that the man should bless him. Jacob said, *"I will not let You go unless You bless me!" (v. 26).* Jacob got the blessing, and his name was changed from Jacob to Israel (v. 29). Jacob and Hannah had got what they desperately wanted due to their insistence demonstrated in their fervent prayer.

These are just a few of many more instances in the bible that underscore the point I am trying to make here. Judging from the examples of these men and women of the Bible, this level of insistence is almost as physically laborious, spiritually engaging and emotionally painful as what the scripture often describes as the *travail of a woman in labor.* The question to you is this: Is there any issue in your life that is driving you to such a point of desperation like Hannah and Jacob? I want to advise that you do not give up because when you persist in prayer, you too would have testimonies of God's faithfulness to share. Since God is not a respecter of persons, neither is He an unresponsive Father, He will hear your knock, open the door of mercy unto you, and bless you according to your heart desire.

You may be wondering how to show such desperation in prayer without pretence, and without making it look like a show or acting. In the next segment, I will explain how you could go about such prayer whenever you have need of it. Most of the things you will read in this segment are made up from my personal experience; and I believe that the same God who heard my knock when I needed to pray this kind of prayer would also hear you.

Knocking in Prayer

As already explained, knocking denotes persistence and insistence. With this in mind, I want you to visualize a

situation that would necessitate you to pray until something happens (PUSH). You may not have the kind of supernatural encounter like Jacob or a priestly intervention like Hannah, but you desperately need a change. Also, you may not have any form of confirmation that your prayer is answered other than the inner witness that God has heard you. The essence of such a prayer is to hang in there tenaciously until you are sure that God has heard you. Let me give you some hints on how to persist in prayer.

1. Separate yourself
This is not the kind of prayer you pray in a hurry, or in the midst of your busy schedule. In such prayer, you must set some time apart to be alone with God. In my own personal experience, any time I decide to pray this kind of prayer, I always separate myself physically by staying away in a secluded place for a number of days without anything that could distract or entangle me with my daily activities like cell phone, laptop, or tablet. In some Christian traditions, people would go to mountain areas dedicated for praying; some would go and stay in hotel rooms, where no one would disturb them, and so on. The point I am making is that this level of praying requires focused attention, the anticipated result of which cannot be attained in a chaotic environment.

2. Pray with fasting
Since it is physically impossible to knock on a door from a distance, it is always advisable to show your tenacity with

fasting. By fasting, your spirit comes up strong, while your body is relatively weakened. In other words, fasting makes your spirit more active and responsive--with clear reception to receive inspirations and revelations from the Holy Spirit-- while your body is weak due to hunger. You may want to know the kind of fast in which you engage yourself, as there are various kinds of fast. My advice is that it does not have to be total fast without food and water, except you are inspired to engage in such a fast. The option is a partial fast in which you abstain from food (and not water) throughout the day, and break your fast in the evening by 6.00 o'clock or at such time as your spirit feels you are ready to break.

3. Prepare adequately
Since knocking involves determination, you must demonstrate your determination by getting your prayer points well prepared before the encounter, based on God's will concerning your situation. This is to enable you to drive your point home without any ambiguity. Everyone who knocks a door is expected to explain why he/she knocks whenever the host shows up. No one knocks another person's door carelessly. Therefore, it is imperative that you get ready to explain your reasons for knocking; and like any other kind of prayer, your reasons must be traceable to the will of God as evident in His Word.

For example, Hannah had a reason for knocking. That was why she was articulate in expressing her heart desire. She did not just ask for a child, but rather clarified her request by asking for a male child who would also be a Nazarene. Hannah even showed the clarity of her request by making the child's destiny part of her request. She wanted a male child who would be of service to God (1 Sam 1:11).

Hannah was aware that her request was in conformity with Gods' will because it is God's will that there should not be any barren in the land (Deut 7:14). The fact that her rival, Peninnah, had children for the same man both of them were married to, shows that her case was not normal, and she needed God's intervention.

4. Pray consistently with the hours of prayer

What I do is to set up prayer sessions every three hours: 6.00am, 9.00am, 12 noon, 3.00pm, 6.00pm, 9.00pm, 12.00 midnight, and 3.00am, making eight prayer sessions altogether in a day of twenty-four hours. The Bible identifies some hours of prayer like when Peter and John went to the temple to pray *"at the hour of prayer, the ninth hour"* (3.00pm) *(Acts 3:1)*. Also the Bible talks about Cornelius who was *"a devout man, and one that feared God . . . and prayed always" (KJV)*. The Bible says that he saw a vision about the ninth hour of the day (3.00pm), which was an hour of prayer. In the same story, Peter was also fasting and praying, and he saw a vision as he prayed *"about the sixth hour"* (12.00noon).

These examples make the biblical injunction clear that *"men always ought to pray and not lose heart" (Lk 18:1)*. This could be done consistent with the hours of prayer. You may be wondering how you could pray consistently every hour for the whole day or days you set aside for the prayer program. Before you are discouraged, let me break down what each prayer hour could consist of. By my own arrangement, I spend the first hour in praise, worship, and prayer; the second hour in reading and meditating on the Word of God; and the third hour for relaxation and light exercise. If you follow such a flexible schedule in your hourly prayer, you would not be easily fagged out and discouraged.

Hearing God's Voice

As earlier expressed, prayer is the art of communing with God, which makes prayer a dialogue and not a monologue. In a dialogue, two people talk together and exchange ideas. So also it is with God. He also wants to talk with you, and show you "great and mighty things, which you do not know" (Jeremiah 33:3). Therefore, for prayer to be complete, we must learn to listen to God, and identify His voice when he speaks. This has been a major missing link in some people's prayer, which I intend to explain in this section so that your prayer would be complete and meaningful. It is expected that every child of God must be able to hear God speak and also identify His voice as distinct from other voices that are always speaking and clogging the mind.

The basic understanding in hearing God is that you should regard it as a spiritual phenomenon and not something physical. Therefore, you should not necessarily expect God to speak to you as a person does, which means that you would not expect to hear God's voice in your ears. May be you have been expecting such a heavy harrowing voice in your ears as you would expect a person talking to you. This may actually be the reason why you have not been hearing His voice because God does not always speak audibly in the ears as a man does except when He wants to. Therefore, since *God is Spirit (Jn 4:24)*, and His Spirit (the Holy Spirit) is on the inside of you, He always communicates with His Spirit who is in you. Since this is a spiritual connection (Spirit to spirit), your natural intellect cannot comprehend what the Spirit is communicating to your spirit. However, for you to comprehend and articulate the communication of the Spirit your spirit transmits the message to your mind, which is the seat of your human understanding and comprehension as it is also the center of decision-making. In this process, the message from your spirit is received in your mind as a thought, an idea, impression, or imagination, which makes it look like God is thinking in you.

As you receive the message in your mind, you might be confused as to who or what is speaking to you because there are some other voices that are also speaking to your mind, like the voice of the devil, and your flesh, otherwise known as your carnal nature. The simple test you could apply in determining the particular voice you are hearing is to determine the quality of the message. Naturally, you would expect God's thought to be superior to your thought, as your mind would not normally produce the kind of thought God thinks to you. He says, *"For my thoughts are not your thoughts, neither are your ways my ways . . ." (Isa 55:8, KJV).*

Thus, when the thought you are "hearing" does not represent your normal thought pattern, that thought is most likely to be from a higher dimension, and you should pay special attention to it as God is thinking to you. Also, the voice of the Holy Spirit is gentle and does not come forcefully. Whenever you hear a voice that comes to you forcefully, in form of a command, that voice is most likely to be the voice of Satan. Another test is the veracity of the thought itself. You have to subject every thought to the provision of the Scripture. If the message contradicts any aspect of God's Word, then the thought is not from God, because God will never contradict Himself, alter or take back whatever He has said (Num 19:30). Lastly, God's thought would always give you peace and not cause you any form of anxiety. Whenever you're not at peace with any thought received in your mind that thought is certainly not from God.

As you regularly hear from God, you would gradually be able to identify His voice. He says, *"And the sheep follow him; for they know his voice" (Jn 10:4).* As you get used to this aspect of prayer, you would discover how exciting and motivational prayer could be. As a matter of fact, you would develop so much intimacy with God that you would always want to be in his presence to communicate with Him. This is what makes praying without ceasing possible. I pray for you that as you explore these areas of persistent prayer, every closed door shall be opened to you, and every secret thing of your life would be brought to light, in Jesus' mighty name.

CHAPTER 4

Level 4: Prayer of Vow

Then she made a vow and said, "O LORD of hosts, if You will indeed look on the affliction of Your maidservant and remember me, and not forget Your maidservant, but will give Your maidservant a male child, then I will give him to the LORD all the days of his life, and no razor shall come upon his head (1 Sam 1:11).

In reality, some people ask, seek, and knock, and yet they do not see the effect of their prayer. What should these people do, since giving up is not an option? When you are in a situation like this, praying the same way as you have been doing would bring the same result, leading to more frustration. Thus, it is important to know how to make your prayer rise to a higher level of intense fervor for the expected result. What in my opinion would make your prayer rise to such a higher level of intense fervor is to make a vow. Although, God does not demand that you should make a vow before your prayer could be answered, when you are in such a critical situation like Hannah, a prayer of vow as quoted above is inevitable.

What is a vow?

For you to make a meaningful vow in your prayer, you must have a clear understanding of what a vow is. The Holman Bible Dictionary defines a vow as "a solemn promise or assertion by which a person binds himself to an act, service or condition." There are two aspects of vows:
1. A vow made explicitly to be offered depending upon the performance of certain favors by God. Examples are; Jacob at Bethel (Gen 28:20-22), and Hannah's dedication of Samuel (1 Sam 1: 11). Such a vow sounds like "God if you do so and so for me, I will give so and so in return as my payment of thanksgiving."
2. The other aspect of vow is the one that is made not as a payment, but more of a commitment. The Bible says about David's commitment to build a house for God,

> *How he swore to the LORD, And vowed to the Mighty One of Jacob: "Surely I will not go into the chamber of my house, Or go up to the comfort of my bed; I will not give sleep to my eyes Or slumber to my eyelids, Until I find a place for the LORD, A dwelling place for the Mighty One of Jacob (Ps 132:2-5).*

Either way, it is obligatory to pay a vow once it is made. The Bible says,

> *When you make a vow to the LORD your God, you shall not delay to pay it; for the LORD your God will*

surely require it of you, and it would be sin to you. But if you abstain from vowing, it shall not be sin to you. That which has gone from your lips you shall keep and perform, for you voluntarily vowed to the LORD your God what you have promised with your mouth (Deut 23:21-23).

Another thing that a vow does is to expose the state of your heart to God; to show whether you love God with all our heart, soul and body, or you love Him for what we intend to get from Him. Thus, when you commit to give up something of value for His faithfulness, it is a demonstration of your love for God. You are also showing that giving up something of value qualifies you for God's blessing. *The Bible says, "Give and it shall be given to you . . ." (Jn 6:38).*

Moreover, a vow could be a reflection of your desire, and the fact that the desire of the righteous shall not be cut off, a vow forms the basis for God's answer to your prayer. For example, Hannah's vow to give back the child she was asking God for ultimately became her desire, which God graciously granted her. Hannah's desire fits in perfectly with God's plan because Samuel eventually became the first prophet in Israel, fulfilling God's plan to cut off the lineage of Eli from the priesthood (1 Sam 2:35). In the Old Testament time, vows were usually made to show the people's faithfulness to God. This is why fulfillment of vows was mandatory.

Biblical examples and evidences of vows redeemed

Hannah made a vow to give back to God the man child she had asked of God all the days of the child's life; and no razor would come on his head (1 Sam 1: 11). It is necessary to find out if Hannah actually fulfilled her vow. The Bible records that when the son, Samuel was weaned (about three years of age), Hannah took him to Eli, the priest, who was regarded as God's representative on earth, to be of service to him. Samuel eventually became the first prophet in Israel. Apart from the fact that God granted Hannah's request ever before she gave Samuel for God's service, the Bible says that Eli blessed Hannah and her husband, Elkanah for fulfilling the vow. *"The LORD give you descendants from this woman for the loan that was given to the LORD" (1 Sam 2:20).* Subsequently, the Lord gave Hannah and her husband three sons and two daughters (v. 21). This is an example of a vow fulfilled, which provoked God's additional blessing.

Another example is Jacob's vow, which he made on his way to sojourn with Laban, after he had escaped from his brother, Esau, who had threatened to kill him for stealing his birthright. On his journey, Jacob came to a place where he dreamed and saw the angels descending and ascending on a ladder whose tip extended to heaven. Jacob recognized the presence of God in the place, which he named Bethel (the house of God). The Bible says that Jacob took the stone that he had used as his pillow, set it up as a pillar, and poured oil on it after which he made a vow,

> *If God will be with me, and will keep me in this way that I go, and will give me bread to eat and clothing to put on, and I come again to my father's house in peace, then shall Jehovah be my God. And this stone which I have set for a pillar shall be God's house. And of all that You shall give me, I will surely give the tenth to You (Gen 28:20-22).*

There is every proof that God was with Jacob, and blessed him abundantly. The Bible says that God also blessed Laban for Jacob's sake (Gen 30:27). However, after twenty years, Jacob decided to return with a large family and a large livestock, and settle in Bethel where he had earlier made a vow. He built an altar there (Gen 35:6), which is an indication that Jacob redeemed his vow because altars were built in those days for offering sacrifice to God. Jacob must have redeemed his vow because the Bible records that God blessed him there and changed his name from Jacob to Israel (v. 10-13).

Jephthah's vow is another example, but with a difference, because it is an example of an unrealistic and unspecified vow for which Jephthah had to pay with his daughter's life. This story is recorded in Judges 11:30ff. Listen to Jephthah's vow,

> *If You will indeed deliver the people of Ammon into my hands, then it will be that **whatever** comes out of the doors of my house to meet me when I return in peace from the people of Ammon, shall surely be the* LORD*'s, and I will*

offer it up as a burnt offering (Judges 11:30-31, emphasis added).

However, on his return from the battle that God made him to win, the unexpected happened: the *whatever* thing that came out first to welcome him was his only daughter. May be Jephthah expected one of his enemies or his dog, or someone not from his close family to come out to welcome him first. Incidentally, his only daughter came out to welcome him. Since a vow cannot be reversed or broken, Jephthah had to sacrifice his only daughter (and only child) as a burnt offering to God.

Although Jephthah's vow was unrealistic, God still remained faithful. It was because of God's faithfulness that Jephthah came back from the battle victorious. Perhaps, he could have lost his life or some terrible things might have happened to him or his troops, but God protected him, and he came back victorious.

Let us look at a biblical example of a vow not honored, and the consequence.. Following Absalom's killing of his brother Amnon who had raped Absalom's sister, Tamar, he absconded from his father for two years, after which Absalom eventually reconciled with his father (1 Sam 15:7ff). He told his father, *"Please let me go to Hebron and pay the vow which I vowed to the Lord. For your servant vowed a vow while I dwell at Geshur in Syria, saying, 'If the Lord indeed brings me back to Jerusalem, then I will serve the Lord'" (vv.7-8).*

God fulfilled His own part of the vow because God brought him back to Jerusalem as Absalom had asked God, but there was no indication that Absalom redeemed his vow to serve the Lord because after David had released Absalom to go and redeem his vow, Absalom decided to plot against his father to overthrow him as king so that he could reign in his father's place. The Bible says in v. 10, (starting the statement with "but"), *"But Absalom sent spies throughout all the tribes of Israel, saying, As soon as you hear the sound of the ram's horn, then you shall say, Absalom reigns in Hebron!" (2 Sam 15:10)*. This is to say that Absalom did not pay his vow. The consequence was severe as Absalom lost his life in the conspiracy that he plotted against his father.

Marriage Vow

In order to bring the issue of vow closer home, let us look at a kind of vow that is familiar and prevalent in our time, which is exchange of vows between a couple in a marriage ceremony. Marriage vow is a kind of vow made between a man and a woman in affirmation of their marriage commitment. Without the exchange of vows, the marriage commitment is not binding on both parties. A typical marriage vow sounds like this,

> I . . . (name) do take thee (name) to be my lawful wedded husband/wife, to have and to hold from this day forward; for better or worse, for richer or poorer, in sickness and in health, to love to cherish, till death do us part according to God's holy ordinance.

Although marriage vow is between couples, it is believed that God is the third party and the unseen witness in the marriage vow, which makes the violation have grievous consequences. The violation is not just against the other party, but also against God. God's involvement in the marriage arrangement makes the marriage institution of great significance unlike what we witnessed in today's marriage, when the sanctity of marriage has been so much eroded that people give different meanings to suit their lustful desires. Thus, marriage vows are not taken seriously any more, as "couples" of the same sex and even of opposite sex are joined together in talk shows, in court houses by unbelievers, and in some "drive through" arrangements. The fact that marriage is an institution established by God, as a union between a man and a woman, makes any other interpretation and vow violation have great consequences.

It is therefore, not a surprise that we have such despicable situations in many homes in our societies today. We witness high rates of divorce, and many children are born out of wedlock, making such children to be raised by single parents. These are, no doubt, some of the consequences of not taking marriage vows seriously, or violating them deliberately. Since the family makes up the society, a broken family would eventually produce a broken society, a broken country, and a broken world.

Conditions of vows in prayer

Like other kinds of prayer, there are conditions for vows made in prayers. Here are some of the conditions:

1. A vow must be paid

As already specified above, vows must be made with all the seriousness it deserves, because it is a commitment that must be paid. A church folksong among the Yoruba tribe of Nigeria interprets to mean that a defaulter of vows is an enemy of God; how could you ever make it into the kingdom of God? A vow is like a debt hanging on the neck of a debtor and until it is paid, it remains a debt. The Bible warns,

> *When you make a vow to God, do not delay to pay it; For He has no pleasure in **fools**. Pay what you have vowed.[5] Better not to vow than to vow and not pay. Do not let your mouth cause your flesh to sin, nor say before the messenger of God that it was an error. Why should God be angry at your excuse and destroy the work of your hands? (Ecc 5:4-6, emphasis added).*

God sees those who make vows and do not pay as fools--*those who witlessly mock him (AMP)*. How would someone mock God and expect to be blessed by the same God that he mocks.

2. A vow must be made with the right motive

The motive behind every vow must be right. This means that it must not be for selfish reasons or for self-gratification. Some people like showing off especially when the vow is made publicly, and in order to impress people, they make vows that they know they cannot possibly pay. You should know that overestimating yourself is a demonstration of your selfish intentions, and such selfish intentions would normally make your prayer ineffective. As the beneficiary of the vow, your focus in prayer should be God, and not yourself. This is why God warns you not to be rash with your mouth (Ecc 5:6).

3. A vow must not be used as a medium of exchange
In every vow, you must understand that you are the beneficiary and not God, as He doesn't need anything from you, neither does He need anything from you before He answers your prayer. Therefore, a vow should not be made to impress God; it should not also be used as a means of exchange for God's favor and blessing. Therefore, you must make your vows with a solemn and humble heart of worship and devotion.

4. A vow must be specific
As hinted above, vows must be paid, and as such, it must be specific. Therefore, before you make a vow, you must give it a second thought to avoid any form of ambiguity. Vows made with good intentions are expected to make your prayer effective, but when your vow makes you feel worse off, it is an unthinkable vow.

5. A vow must be realistic
Just as a vow must be specific, it must also be realistic. Jephthah's vow did not also pass the test of reality and genuineness. Offering his only daughter was not the most reasonable thing to do under the circumstance of winning a battle. Therefore, whenever you are making a vow, avoid making it under pressure, in a hurry or in a vague manner. Rather, make sure you give yourself ample time to think over the vow so that you would not regret making an unrealistic one.

6. A vow must make a demand on you

The fact that you should make a specific and a realistic vow does not give you the liberty to make a vow, as simple as to border on a lack of seriousness. Such a vow could be categorized as unrealistic. Listen to an example of an unserious vow, "God, if you give me success in my endeavor, I will dance and celebrate on your altar, and before the congregation." What makes this vow unrealistic is its simplicity, because dancing and celebrating before the Lord are normal and regular acts of service, which do not normally cost the person anything. Thus, your vow must put a specific and an uncommon demand on you as an evidence of your seriousness and commitment.

In conclusion, no matter the urgency, and the seriousness of the issue at stake, it is necessary to make vows that you could fulfill. Remember that God's yoke is always easy, and His burden is normally light (Matt 11:29-30). Therefore, do not place an unnecessary burden on yourself as you decide to make a vow for the effectiveness of your prayer.

CHAPTER 5

Level 5: Prayer Mingled with Tears

And she was in bitterness of soul, and prayed to the LORD and wept in anguish. (1 Sam 1:10).

There are some situations that would make you shed tears as you pray. Hannah was in such a situation because the Bible says that she wept in anguish. It is evident from this passage that Hannah did not just shed ordinary emotional tears, but wept due to the bitterness of her soul. As a matter of fact, God would not have been moved by Hannah's emotional tears because God is not like a man who could be swayed by emotions.

Kinds of Tears

In my findings, I discover five different kinds of tears as recorded in the Scriptures.

1. Tears of Sadness.
This is the kind of tears shed at the loss of a loved one. The grief and sorrow involved in the loss would naturally make the grieving person shed tears of sorrow. A biblical example is when David and his men came back to their camp and discovered that the Amelekite army had ransacked their camp, burnt it down, and went away with their wives and children (1 Sam 30:1-20). The Bible described their sorrow to be of such intensity that they wept until they had no more power to weep (v. 5). It is possible that you are experiencing this kind of sorrow for the loss of a loved one. I pray that God, the Comforter, will comfort and give you the strength to bear your loss.

2. Tears of penitence
These are the kinds of tears shed when a sinner is convicted of his/her sins, and seeks God's mercy for forgiveness. Such tears are the expression of the sinner's contrition and repentance. This is not to say that every sinner has to shed tears to be forgiven their sins, or that they cannot experience God's forgiveness unless they shed tears of penitence. The important thing is their conviction, which could be expressed in any way possible. If you have not experienced such conviction that leads to repentance, I urge you to accept Jesus' sacrifice on the cross of Calvary, and be cleansed of

your sins to become a born again child of God. The Bible says of the sinful woman who stood at Jesus' feet weeping, as she wetted his feet with her tears, dried them with her hair and, robbed them with perfume. Although her action was condemned by the Pharisees, Jesus commended her, and forgave her sin. Jesus said to his host,

> *Then He turned to the woman and said to Simon, "Do you see this woman? I entered your house; you gave Me no water for My feet, but* **she has washed My feet with her tears** *and wiped them with the hair of her head. You gave Me no kiss, but this woman has not ceased to kiss My feet since the time I came in. You did not anoint My head with oil, but this woman has anointed My feet with fragrant oil. Therefore I say to you, her sins, which are many are forgiven, for she loved much. But to whom little is forgiven, the same loves little." Then He said to her, "Your sins are forgiven" (Lk 7:44-48, emphasis added).*

3. Tears of passion

The tears you shed when a situation makes you angry is an indication of the problem God has called you to solve. Mike Murdock writes, "What grieves you is a clue to what you are assigned to heal"[4] The Bible says about Nehemiah when he heard the news of the deplorable condition of the people left behind in Jerusalem, and the dilapidated walls of the city following the Babylonian captivity of Judah, *"So it was, when I heard these words, that I sat down and* **wept, and mourned** *for many days; I was fasting and praying before* *the God of heaven" (Neh 1:4, emphasis added)*. The tears that flow from your eyes when you are passionate about a situation like that of Nehemiah is regarded as tears of passion which is a pointer to God's assignment for you. Mike Murdock added, "What makes you cry is a clue to the problem God has qualified you to heal."[5]

4. Tears of joy
There are times when you feel so elated and excited about a situation that the joy of it makes you shed some tears. These are tears that Prophet Jeremiah talks about when he prophesied:

> *Tears of joy will stream down their faces, and I will lead them home with great care. They will walk beside quiet streams and on smooth paths where they will not stumble. For I am Israel's father, and Ephraim is my oldest child (Jer. 31:9)*

That is what I regard as tears of joy.

5. Tears of grief and anguish
The kind of tears I am emphasizing in the context of this book is the tears of grief and anguish. Let me give some Scriptural illustrations. The Bible says about Hannah that *"she was in bitterness of soul, and prayed to the LORD and wept in anguish" (1 Sam 1:10)*. This kind of bitterness originates in the soul, which is usually deeper than physical or emotional pain. Apart from the fact that Hannah was in bitterness due to her condition of childlessness, Peninnah's provocation was another cause of her suffering and anguish. The Bible says that Peninnah *"provoked her severely, to make her miserable" (v. 8)*. Peninnah's provocation and humiliation must have caused Hannah so much bitterness that

she wept and lost her appetite. The fact that their husband favored Hannah in the distribution of the yearly portion over Peninnah who had sons and daughters for him could also make Peninnah so jealous that she might decide to take it out on Hannah what she considered as the husband's partiality.

Another example is when God sent prophet Isaiah to tell Hezekiah to put his house in order and prepare to die because he was not going to recover from his ailment. The Bible says, *"Hezekiah wept bitterly" (Isa 38:3)*. God heard his prayer, and Hezekiah was healed of his sickness and God prolonged his life by fifteen years. God told him, *"I have heard your prayer, I have seen your tears; surely I will add to your days fifteen years" (Isa 38:5)*. God mentioned specifically that He had seen Hezekiah's tears, which he shed in his prayer.

A friend once shared his experience with me. It has the resemblance of Hannah and Hezekiah's condition. He revealed that when he lost his job, and could not provide for his family, he did not feel the pain of the loss of his job as much as the provocation of his in-laws who ridiculed and made fun of him. According to my friend, his in-laws humiliated him so much that they told him to his face that he was not better than a servant in the house. They even sarcastically referred to him as the *wife* of the house as he could not perform the basic responsibility of a husband. My friend recalled how he was always moved to tears any time he was praying, which he said was caused not by the loss of his job, but by the taunting and provocation of his in-laws. However, just like Hannah, this friend's situation had a happy ending because he eventually got a job that was even better than the one he lost, and his situation drastically changed for the better. Job wrote about his similar condition, *"My friends scorn me; My eyes pour out tears to God" (Job 16:20).*

Shortly before Jesus was crucified, He prayed in anguish in the Garden of Gethsemane. The Bible says, *"And being in agony, He prayed more earnestly. Then His sweat became like great drops of blood falling down to the ground" (Lk 22:44).* Although the writer of this Gospel regarded what was dropping from Jesus' body as *sweat*, the writer of the Book of Hebrews regarded it as tears. *"Who, in the days of His flesh, when He had offered up prayers and supplications, with vehement cries and **tears** to Him who was able to save Him from death, and was heard because of His godly fear" (Heb 5:7, emphasis added).* Although Jesus felt the anguish and pain, but *"for the joy that was set before Him endured the cross, despising the shame, and has sat down at the right hand of the throne of God" (Heb 12:2).* Jesus eventually went to the cross, a painful obedience that made it possible for God's plan of redemption to be carried out for mankind. Paul also wrote of his feeling of disappointment and sorrowful emotion in his epistle to the church of Corinth, concerning the report of fornication in the church. He said, *"For out of much affliction and anguish of heart I wrote to you, with many tears" (2 Cor 2:4).*

There are some situations that would make you not to hold back your tears when you are making supplications to God. Such tears that flow from a sorrowful heart are not usually unnoticed. The Bible reveals that God has a record of such tears. *"You number my wanderings; Put my tears into Your bottle; Are they not in Your book?" (Ps 56:8).* See Henry Matthew comments on this Scripture, "God always hears the prayers of the broken in the heart, and will give health, length of days, and temporary deliverance as much and as long as it is truly good for them."

There is enough evidence to prove that God always hears the prayers of the broken-hearted. The Bible usually expresses the tears of the broken hearted as something that puts God in remembrance of their situation, and causes changes in their situation. This is not to say that God is forgetful, and therefore, needs to be reminded of His promises before He could act. Rather, it is a way of describing God's reaction in the human or natural sense for proper understanding. For instance, Hezekiah prayed, *"Remember now . . ." (Isa 38:3).* Hannah also prayed, *"Remember me and not forget your handmaid . . ." (1 Sam 1:11).* It is on record that God remembered both of them, and turned their situations around. These are evidences of prayer mingled with tears being heard by God. However, like other kinds of prayers, there are some conditions that must be fulfilled for such prayers to be answered. Here are some of the conditions.

Conditions for Prayer with Tears

1. Avoid being outwardly emotional
When an adult cries like a baby who wants the attention of his parents, it would not make your prayer effective. Rather, the tear you shed as a result of the anguish and suffering that weigh so heavily in your heart, is what is capable of bringing about some effect on your prayer. The Bible says, *"The earnest (heartfelt, continued) prayer of a righteous man makes tremendous power available (dynamic in its working)*

(Jms 5:16, AMP). When the heart is broken or in anguish, and tears flow from such a heart in prayer, it makes God react compassionately to you, and attend to your prayer. This is quite different from any other kind of tears. In fact, I would advise that you do not pray when you are superficially emotional. Let such an emotion run out before praying because it could be a hindrance to your prayer focus.

2. Praying with a clean heart

Since the condition of your heart is what makes the difference in this kind of payer, it follows that you must maintain a clean heart in this as in other kinds of prayer. There are certain things that could jeopardize your prayer if care is not taken. For instance, your heart must not harbor the work of the flesh like anger, unforgiveness, and resentment.

When Hezekiah was in a serious predicament, the Bible says that he cited his work with God with a perfect heart as a testimony, *"Remember now, O LORD, I pray, how I have walked before You in truth and with a loyal heart, and have done what is good in Your sight" (Isa 38:3)*. Since every heart is before God like an open book, it is essential that you do not allow those things that could make your heart unclean because they could hinder your prayer, and make your tears of no effect. The Bible says specifically that God hears the prayer of the righteous, and those who do God's will. *"Now we know that God does not hear sinners; but if anyone is a worshiper of God and does His will, He hears him" (Jn 9:31)*.

3. Absolute trust in God

When praying this kind of prayer, there should not be any design that would make you feel that if God fails, you have an alternative plan. Your position should be that of, "if God decides not to do it, let it remain undone." This is a point of no return. This is the point in which Hannah and Hezekiah found themselves that made them pray tenaciously and be adamantly determined to receive God's blessing.

4. Have an intimate relationship with God

This is not the kind of prayer that you just stumble into. Rather, you work your way into it based on your intimate relationship with God. Apart from being a child of God, which is an essential condition for all prayers, your intimate relationship with Him should not be in doubt. This is what Hezekiah based his prayer on as he prayed, *"Remember now, O LORD, I pray, how I have walked before You in truth and with a loyal heart, and have done what is good in Your sight" (Isa 38:3).* What Hezekiah meant when he said, "I have walked before thee," is that apart from boasting of his righteousness before God, he is also reflecting on his intimacy with God.

Here are challenging questions you need to answer in your heart: Do you have any evidence of intimacy in your relationship with God? Do you abide in Him and does His Word abide in you? The Lord Himself said, *"If you abide in Me, and My words abide in you, you will ask what you desire, and it shall be done for you" (Jn 15:7).* Not many people have the testimony of prayer mingled with tears since this is not expected to be a voluntary emotional reaction. It is also possible that your situation is not as serious as to make you tearful. However, I hope that you understand the implications of such prayer so that you would know how to go about it whenever the situation arises.

It is quite possible that after you have prayed some earnest prayers to God for some specific need, based on the will of God, and you receive no answer from heaven, it means that there is need for you to step up your prayer to the next level. This is the level of Prayer with fasting to obtain.

CHAPTER 6

Level 6: Prayer with Fasting to Obtain

> *So it was, year by year, when she went up to the house of the* LORD*, that she provoked her; therefore she wept and **did not eat**... So the woman went her way **and ate**, and her face was no longer sad (1 Sam 1:7- 18, emphasis added).*

In Hannah's predicament, the Bible says that she did not eat. Although the Bible does not state specifically that Hannah fasted, it is evident that her not eating as she prayed represents a state of fasting. More so, the Bible states that she decided to eat after she had prayed alone with God. This could mean that she decided to break her fast believing that her prayer has been answered. Thus, when you decide to complement your prayer with fasting in order to obtain a desired result, it is a different level of prayer entirely which I refer to as Prayer with fasting to obtain. This is the focus of this chapter.

What is a Fast?

There are different applications to the concept of fasting because people give different meanings to it. Somebody asked me some time ago if he could fast by abstaining from watching the television for some days. Another person regarded her not putting on her makeup for a number of days as *fasting*. It becomes more complicated when other religions claim to fast as part of their religious rites. Therefore, I will explain in this section what biblical fasting represents.

Although abstaining from other things for a period of time is a sort of self-denial, the basic understanding of fasting in the Scriptures and in the content of this book is, refraining from eating food. It is not just refraining from food as if one is starving or on a hunger strike, but refraining from food for a specific period of time to enable the person become more intense in his/her prayer. Thus, for a fast to be effective, it must be accompanied by prayer, and meditating on the Word of God. Fasting is designed to make prayer mount up as on eagle's wings. It is calculated to give an edge to a man's intercessions and power to his petition. Heaven is ready to bend its ears to listen when someone prays with fasting.

Forms of fasting

There are three forms of fasting specified in the Bible. First is normal fast, which involves abstinence from food for a number of days, but not from water. An example is Jesus' fast. The Bible says, *"And in those days He ate nothing, and afterward, when they had ended, He was hungry" (Lk 4:2).* The understanding is that Jesus abstained from food but not water. Second is absolute fast, which involves total abstinence from food and water. An example is Paul's fast after his conversion. He neither eat nor drink (Acts 9:9). Esther also fasted with her people without food or water for three nights and days (Est 4:16). This kind of fast does not usually last for long--usually three days. Third is partial fast with emphasis on restriction rather than abstinence. An example is Daniel's fast in which he *"ate no pleasant food, no meat or wine came into my mouth, nor did I anoint myself at all, till three whole weeks were fulfilled" (Dan 10:3).* This kind of fast could last for as long as the person desires. For Daniel, it lasted for twenty-one days. Within the period, Daniel received the end-time revelation for Israel in what is usually referred to as The vision of Seventy Weeks as recorded in Dan 9:24-27.

Purposes of Fasting

There are times that your situations would necessitate seeking God more intently. In such a situation, you could give support to your prayer by fasting. One of the various reasons for fasting specified in the Bible is to give effect to our prayer, by making our voice heard in heaven. This assertion supports the fact that prayer is a weapon of warfare. In prayer, we wrestle against opposing forces of darkness, and spiritual cross-currents which are antagonistic to God's purpose for our lives. The Bible says, *"For we do not wrestle against flesh and blood, but against principalities, against powers, against the rulers of the darkness of this age, against spiritual hosts of wickedness in the heavenly places" (Eph 6:12).*

Therefore, confronting such spiritual forces in warfare would naturally take more than regular prayer to accomplish, but should also include fasting. Moreover, fasting enables one to seek God more intently. This is what God expressed when He said, *"When you seek me with all your heart, I will be found by you" (Jere 29:13).* Seeking God with all of one's heart could mean setting aside the legitimate appetites of the body to concentrate on praying. The person is demonstrating that he/she is seeking with his/her heart, and would not relent unless God answers.

God says through Prophet Joel, "Now, therefore," says the LORD, *"Turn to Me with all your heart, With fasting, with weeping, and with mourning" (Joel 2:12).* There is no doubt that fasting makes tremendous impact when we fast and pray. Arthur Wallis writes, "Fasting is calculated to bring a note of urgency and importunity into our praying, and to give force to our pleading in the court of heaven."[6]

Fasting is a formidable weapon in empowering our prayer for divine intervention. The Bible records an incident in which the Benjamites committed a terrible crime, and God instructed the other tribes to go against them. The other tribes did what God instructed them to do, but were heavily defeated both times. However, on the third occasion, they fasted and went before God, and God gave them victory (Judges 20). This is what fasting to obtain signifies. It also shows that obtaining God's promises must not be taken for granted, because the other tribes instructed to attack could assume that since they were acting on God's instruction, their victory was sure, yet they suffered defeat. This is to show that the promises of God are obtainable when we are serious and desperate to have them in prayer and fasting.

Wallis wrote, "Even if heaven had issued the decree and the wheels are already in motion, there is still a mighty weapon to which we can have recourse."[7] That mighty weapon is prayer and fasting. I have seen people deciding to fast randomly, and at will. Some other people pray randomly with fasting. However, fasting to obtain must be targeted at some specific needs for which you want your prayer to effect. This is to say that, for your prayer with fasting to be effective, you don't just stumble into it, but plan it carefully with relevant Scriptural prayers. In some cases, God could inspire such a fast, specifying the number of days you're to fast. This is what makes such a fast effective and meaningful.

Conditions for an Acceptable Fast

Not every fast is acceptable before God, otherwise God would not have reminded us that the acceptable fast is the one He has chosen (Isa 58:6). Let us look at the kind of fast that God has chosen, and the conditions for such a fast.

1. Fasting unto God
"When you fasted and mourned . . . did you really fast for Me—for Me?" (Zech 7:5). The motive behind a fast is as important as the fast itself. In fact, fasting with a wrong motive could rob it of its intended benefits. Thus, for your fast to be effective and acceptable, it must not be motivated

by self-interest and desire for things. Rather, your fast must be intended to honor and glorify God, so that *"your Father who sees in secret will reward you openly" (Matt 6:6).*

An example of fasting for self gratification is cited in the Scriptures as that of the Pharisee *"who prayed thus with himself, 'God, I thank You that I am not like other men . . . I fast twice a week; I give tithes of all that I possess.'" (Lk 18:11-12).* The Pharisee was praying to himself, and not to God, whereas a meaningful prayer and fasting is expected to honor and minister to the Lord like the apostles' fast. The Bible says, *"As they **ministered to the Lord and fasted,** the Holy Spirit said, "Now separate to Me Barnabas and Saul for the work to which I have called them"(Acts 13:2, emphasis added).* This is probably why God responded by giving them specific instructions on the direction of their ministry. The apostles responded by fasting and praying again, after which they laid hands on Paul and Barnabas, and then let them go (v.3).

2. A fast must be inspired

You do not fast just because you want to fast. Rather, you fast because you have such a burden to do so. Fasting like prayer is a spiritual obligation, because Jesus says in His Sermon on the Mount, "When you pray;" "when you fast" (Matt 6:5,16). This makes fasting as well as prayer obligatory and not optional. However, fasting like prayer must be God-initiated and God-inspired if it is to be effective. God normally places a burden on us by His Spirit, and it is our responsibility to respond positively to such a burden. Wallis says, "Prayer that originates with God always returns to God. So it is with fasting"[8] A fast initiated by God would normally specify when to fast, how long to fast, the nature of the fast, and the spiritual objective to be attained, all for the purpose of accomplishing God's sovereign will. It is our responsibility to be obedient and disciplined in our response, and the God who sees in secret is more than able to reward us openly.

3. Fasting must not be for outward showing

> *Moreover, when you fast, do not be like the hypocrites, with a sad countenance. For they disfigure their faces that they may appear to men to be fasting. Assuredly, I say to you, they have their reward. But you, when you fast, anoint your head and wash your face, so that you do not appear to men to be fasting, but to your Father who is in the secret place; and your Father who sees in secret will reward you openly (Matt 6:16-18).*

This is a profound teaching on our appearance and motive when fasting. Jesus' teaching specifies that anyone who fasts for the purpose of impressing others or for self-gratification has no benefit with God. Someone once announced to me, with excitement and unsolicited that he had been fasting for twenty-eight days, and he had twelve days to go. I then asked him what he wanted me to do with such information to which he responded that he just wanted me to know. After telling him that the information was of no benefit to me, I reminded him that he should let his fasting be a personal thing between him and God, because he expected the reward from God and mot from man. He got the message, and did not inform me of his fasting any more since then. Therefore, fasting being a spiritual exercise must be taken seriously and must not be done to impress other people for it to be effective and acceptable.

Chapter 7

Level 7: Prayer with Sacrifice

> *There was a certain man in Caesarea called Cornelius, a centurion of what was called the Italian Regiment, ² a devout man and one who feared God with all his household,* **who gave alms generously to the people, and prayed to God always**. *. . So he said to him,* **"Your prayers and your alms have come up for a memorial before God** *(Acts 10:1-4, emphasis added).*

The seventh and final level of prayer is prayer with sacrifice. It is necessary to understand the concept of sacrifice in this context, as against the common understanding of animal and blood sacrifice. In the Old Testament time, animal and blood sacrifice was an acceptable mode of worship because God specifically demanded such sacrifice on a daily, monthly and ceremonial basis. Sacrifice then was regarded as a physical expression of the people's inward devotion. While God does not change, and still accepts sacrifice, there has been a dramatic shift from the Old Testament practice to a different mode of worship. This is the focus of this chapter.

The Obsolesce of Animal Sacrifice

With the sacrifice that Jesus paid on the cross of Calvary, the Bible ascertains that no other sacrifice is required any more for the forgiveness of sin. *"But this Man, after He had offered one sacrifice for sins forever, sat down at the right hand of God" (Heb 7:12).* Christ is the Lamb without blemish who was offered as a sacrifice for sinners (Heb 7:27). This is why Christians should not be involved in any form of fetish sacrifice usually practiced by other religions to appease their gods because such sacrifice is usually designed for the worship of the devil. Also, you should be wary of any prophet who demands for money or materials for sacrifice to appease some gods as the solution to your problem.

Qualifications to Offer Sacrifice

The Bible says that Christ has made us priests and kings unto God (Rev 5:10). Therefore, as priests and kings, believers have the responsibility of offering some sort of sacrifice to God, because it is the responsibility of the priest to intercede for the people. The Bible says,

> *"But you are a chosen generation, a royal priesthood, a holy nation, His own special people, that you may proclaim the praises of Him who called you out of darkness into His marvelous light" (1 Pet 2:9).*

Thus, every believer has the spiritual responsibility to intercede for his or her family, group, church, or nation. Also, as believers we are the temple of the Holy Spirit, and as such we have the responsibility to offer acceptable sacrifice in form of our reasonable service (1 Cor 3:16).

Apostle Peter describes believers as *"living stones, being built up a spiritual house, a holy priesthood, to offer up spiritual sacrifices acceptable to God through Jesus Christ" (1 Pet 2:5).* This gives us the understanding that believers are qualified to offer sacrifice to God in the following ways: First, as we reflect the holiness of God; second, as we offer spiritual sacrifice; third, as we intercede for others before God; and lastly, as we present God before others. Arthur Wallis puts it this way, "Under the old covenant God had a temple for His people; under the new covenant God has His people for a temple."[9]

Thus, a sacrifice does not need to be animal or blood sacrifice to be acceptable to God. A sacrifice is described as "Whatever is offered to God by man as a means of attesting to the greatness of God"[10] With this understanding, anything offered to God in form of offering, gifts, and devotion could be regarded as a sacrifice. It is in this context we are considering *sacrifice* in this book.

Kinds of Sacrifice

The specific sacrifice the Bible refers to as acceptable and as our reasonable service is the sacrifice we offer to God through our worship. Let me identify three of such sacrifices. First, offering of money and material things. Paul describes this kind of offering which the Philippian church gave him as *"a fragrant offering, an acceptable sacrifice, pleasing to God" (Phil 4:18, NIV)*. Therefore, when you give money or material things with the heart of worship, you are offering an acceptable sacrifice to God. Second, sacrifice of praise. It is often said that whenever praise goes up, blessings come down. This is to confirm that praise is a sacrifice that is able to procure God's blessings as it is offered with the heart of worship. The Bible says, *"Therefore by Him let us continually offer the sacrifice of praise to God, that is, the fruit of our lips, giving thanks to His name" (Heb 13:15)*. Third, sacrifice of good works. This is the basis of our Christian faith because we are called into good works. The Bible says, *"For we are His workmanship, created in Christ Jesus for good works, which God prepared beforehand that we should walk in them" (Eph 2:10)*. We are also redeemed into good works, (Tit 2:14). This is why giving to the poor is regarded as a sacrifice (Acts 10:4).

Since sacrifice involves giving of money and material things, I want to emphasize three kinds of giving, in support of prayer. These are:

1. Battle seed offering
2. Thanksgiving offering, and
3. Sacrificial offering.

These three offerings are meant to express your earnest determination to receive answer to our prayer. Most times, it is not even the offering, but your obedience that makes the difference. Let us consider the application of these offerings in relation to prayer.

1. Battle seed offering

As the name implies, this is a sacrificial offering given when one faces an overwhelming and formidable battle of life. The offering is regarded as a seed because it has the same characteristics of a physical seed. A seed is a living organism, and the life of the plant is in the seed. This is why the seed of a plant produces its kind--an apple seed will always produce an apple fruit, and not orange. Another quality of a seed is its ability to multiply. In other words, an apple seed has the potential to produce multiples of apple fruits. However, for the seed to produce and multiply, it must be sown. The Bible says, "Unless a grain of wheat falls into the ground and dies, it remains alone; but if it dies, it produces much grain" (Jn 12:24). Thus, just as a seed sown has the potential to multiply, so also the offering offered as a seed has the potential to multiply in benefits concerning the situation for which it is given.

A battle seed offering is regarded as a sacrifice because, as said above, it is meant to attest to God's greatness. The fact that giving the offering denies you of the benefits you could have derived from using the money for other things makes it a sacrifice. However, as the money leaves your hand, it does not leave your life, but goes into your future. When you give a battle seed offering towards a life situation, it is intended to express your earnestness in sacrificing, attesting to God's greatness over the situation. A battle seed offering could be inspired, and you could be prompted to give a specific offering. I recall a situation I was confronted with concerning a business transaction that did not show any prospect of succeeding. As I prayed, I had the nudge to give a battle seed offering so that the transaction would come out with benefits.

I gave the offering, and the unusual but expected happened. The partner who was not cooperating, and wanted to dupe me of my share called to offer me what I deserved. I knew instantly that it was not a coincidence but a confirmation that my sacrificial offering had made the difference.

2. Thanksgiving offering

Thanksgiving could be defined as expression of gratitude for the blessings enjoyed through God's goodness and faithfulness, including the gift of redemption. The Bible says, *"Every good gift and every perfect gift is from above, and comes down from the Father of lights, with whom there is no variation or shadow of turning" (Jm 1:17)*. Therefore, with God at the center of every gift pertaining to us, it is expedient for us to always give thanks to Him. The Bible says, *"In everything give thanks; for this is the will of God in Christ Jesus for you" (1 Thess 5:18)*. Many of these gifts are not quantifiable as they are not physical. For instance, the benefit of God's protection against accidents cannot be quantified, especially when some of the accidents are divinely averted without us knowing it.

An example of such thanksgiving of personal and even national deliverance is expressed by David, *"You have put gladness in my heart, More than in the season that their grain and wine increased. I will both lie down in peace, and sleep; For You alone, O LORD, make me dwell in safety" (Ps 4:7-8)*. Therefore, thanksgiving is a natural element of Christian worship and is expected to characterize all of our Christian life. When you give an offering of thanksgiving, you are not only showing your appreciation in a more meaningful way, you are also making the blessing irreversible, while showing that you deserve more of such blessings.

It is easy and natural to express thanksgiving for blessings already experienced, but it is not common to express appreciation for blessings not yet experienced. However, when you show such appreciation for anticipated blessings in advance, you are exercising your faith, believing that what God has promised, He would do, and as a result, you are moving God into action because He is always moved by faith.

3. Sacrificial offering

Whatever you give out of your possessions that places a demand on you, and is aimed at honoring God is a sacrificial offering. Let us look at a biblical example of Cornelius, a captain of the Italian band, who was described as *"a devout man and one who feared God with all his household,* ***who gave alms generously to the people,*** *and prayed to God always" (Act 10:1, emphasis added).* Cornelius was a man of prayer, who was always giving alms to the poor. As he was praying one day, an angel of God appeared to him, saying: *"Your prayer and your generous gifts to the poor have come up (as a sacrifice) to God and have been remembered by Him" (Acts 10:4, AMP).* God then told Cornelius what to do as an answer to his prayer, and consequently, he and his household became the first gentile family to receive the gift of the Holy Spirit (10:44).

Many people pray earnestly, but very few know how to support their prayer with sacrificial giving. God did not just hear Cornelius' prayer, but his alms also came up to God as a sacrifice, which made God to remember him. Thus, the combination of prayer and sacrifice makes up a strong appeal for God's intervention. The Word of God attests to this, *"He who has a generous eye will be blessed, For he gives of his bread to the poor" (Prov 22:9).* Therefore, giving to the poor has God's connection to it because the Bible says, *"He who has pity on the poor lends to the LORD, And He will pay back what he has given" (Prov 19:17).*

Think of Solomon's sacrificial burnt offering, in which he sacrificed one thousand animals to God (1 Kings 3:1-5). The sacrifice served as a catalyst to greater blessings, especially because Solomon was motivated by his love for God. Apart from the wealth and riches that God promised and gave Solomon, God also gave him peace in his kingdom more than any other king, either before or after him.

Another example is Hannah who vowed to God concerning a male child that was her heart desire. She vowed that if God should give her a male child, she would lend him to God all the days of his life, and no razor shall tough his hair (1 Sam 11). Hannah fulfilled her vow because when Samuel was about three years old, she took him to Eli, the priest to serve in the house of the Lord. Some people might feel that giving up Samuel for God's service was too simple to be regarded as a sacrifice. I want to advise such people to put themselves in Hannah's shoes, or ask any mother how emotionally painful and demanding it could be to part with a three year old son.

Apart from being the only son, the mother's emotional detachment could be indescribable. This is why I believe that Hannah's sacrifice of giving Samuel for God's service was a catalyst that provoked other blessings. The Bible says that as many times as Hannah and her husband went to Shiloh to worship, Eli the priest would bless them, "And Eli would bless Elkanah and his wife, and say, *"The LORD give you descendants from this woman for the loan that was given to the LORD"* (1 Sam 2:20). As a result, Hannah was blessed with five other children, three male, and two female (v. 22). This means that God responded to her sacrifice by giving her more children. Is there anything barren in your life for which you are seeking God's intervention? You could follow the biblical examples cited in this section, by offering a qualitative offering that would cost you something to God who is more than able to respond positively to your sacrifice, and grant you more than you desire. When you give your best offering with the heart of love, expect God's mighty hand to move in your favor.

Conditions for an Acceptable Sacrifice

There is no doubt that God honors a sacrifice when it is properly presented. Considering the example of Abel and Cain who presented different kinds of sacrifice, the Bible says that God accepted Abel's sacrifice, but rejected that of Cain (Gen 4:1-5). This is to confirm that there are some sacrifices that could be rejected because they do not qualify for God's acceptance. Look at how the Bible presents God's reaction to both Abel and Cain's sacrifices, *"And God respected Abel and his offering" (v. 4),* while *"He did not respect Cain and his offering" (v. 5).* "Having respect" means *look with favor (NIV).* This is to say that Abel's sacrifice provoked God's blessing, while that of Cain did not.

Apart from the theological explanation of God's reaction to both Abel and Cain's sacrifice, the writer of Hebrews emphasizes the attitude and motive with which each of them offered their sacrifice, which was said to be the basis of God's reaction. The Bible says,

> *"By faith Abel offered to God a more excellent sacrifice than Cain, through which he obtained witness that he was righteous, God testifying of his gifts; and through it he being dead still speaks" (Heb 11:4).*

This is to say that Abel's sacrifice was offered by faith and this made it acceptable. It was for this that his was considered righteous, while that of Cain was in doubt, thereby his sacrifice was unacceptable. Therefore a sacrifice must satisfy some conditions for its acceptability. Consider below some of the conditions for an acceptable offering:

1. Giving with the right motive
The motive with which you present your offering is very important in determining its acceptability or a lack thereof. Thus, what is the thought behind your mind in giving your offering? Are you motivated by what you are going to benefit from the offering, or by your love for God? While every giver has the natural tendency to think of the purpose for giving the offering, the overriding intention must be out of your love for God, otherwise it would look like you are exchanging your offering for God's blessing, which you cannot possibly buy with money. Moreover, a self-centered motive makes it look like you are doing God some favor. As you know, God does not need your offering for His own

benefit, because the source of the sacrifice and everything you have, is from God (Psalm 50). This is also why you must consider nothing too big to be given as sacrifice to God.

2. Giving with the right attitude

The attitude with which you give is also important because it determines the acceptability of your giving. For instance, when you give as if you are compelled to do so, and behave as if God is robbing you of your possession, such a sacrifice is with a negative attitude, and could rob you of the benefits. The Bible says:

> *Let each one (give) as he has made up his own mind and purposed in his heart, not reluctantly or sorrowfully or under compulsion, for God loves (He takes pleasure in, prizes above other things, and is unwilling to abandon or to do without) a cheerful (joyful, "prompt to do it") giver (whose heart is in his giving)." (2 Cor 9:7, AMP).*

A cheerful giver is considered to be the person who is joyful in giving, whose heart is in his/her giving, and who is prompted to give. Such a person would not have any feeling of compulsion or reluctance. God takes pleasure in givers with such attitude. Therefore, every offering you give must be voluntary, and must be given cheerfully. As a matter of fact, the underlining meaning of sacrifice involves voluntary and cheerful giving.

There are some lessons to learn from Abraham in respect of sacrificial giving. When God called Abraham, the Bible says that he built an altar unto the Lord (Gen 12:7). As he journeyed from the place, he built another altar, where the Bible says, *"He called on the name of the Lord" (Gen 12:7 - 13:8; 22:9)*. Abraham's motive for building the altars wherever he went even when he was not compelled to do so was to offer sacrifice to God because there cannot be an altar without a sacrifice. This is why it did not take Abraham time to put together all the materials he would need, as he built an altar to sacrifice Isaac as burnt offering when God told him to do so. (Gen 22:1). There is no doubt that Abraham's motive was right, and this is why God counted it to him as righteousness. Listen to God's blessings following Abraham's sacrifice of Isaac as He declared:

> *By Myself I have sworn, says the LORD, because you have done this thing, and have not withheld your son, your only son— [17] blessing I will bless you, and multiplying I will multiply your descendants as the stars of the heaven and as the sand which is on the seashore; and your descendants shall possess the gate of their enemies. [18] In your seed all the nations of the earth shall be blessed, because you have obeyed My voice (Gen 22:16-18).*

This is to show that God could demand a sacrifice from you as a way of testing your faith in and love for Him. However, whenever God makes such a demand, it is certain that He has some blessings ready for your act of obedience. I pray that you don't miss such blessings any time you are prompted to give offering of any kind to God.

3. Giving a high quality offering

Your offering to the Most High God must be of the highest quality. This is why the quality of sacrifice in the Old Testament was specified. For instance, Malachi wrote about the quality of the people's offering which he said was detestable as they were offering blind and lame animals to God (Mal 1:13-14). Similarly, the quality of what we offer to God is expected to be of the highest standard. For instance, it is not a good practice to give the leftover of your money as offering and tithe, after you have settled your other bills that you think are of more importance to you. However, when you give God first out of your pay check or income, that offering is considered as of great value because it is motivated by your love for God which makes you want to regard Him first. When you give this way, you are qualified for open windows of heaven through which God promises to pour down His blessings that you would not have enough room to take them in (Mal 3:8-10).

4. Your sacrifice must cost you something

An offering that costs you something is one that makes a great demand on you. For instance, an offering that you give out of your income represents the sweat of your labor produced from the blood and fluid that flows through your veins. This makes such an offering a sacrifice that costs you something.

David shows an example of such a sacrifice when Prophet Gad told him to *"erect an altar to the LORD on the threshing floor of Araunah the Jebusite" (2 Sam 24:18).* This sacrifice was intended to appease God in the killing of the Israelites following David's conduct of a census of the people. Araunah the owner of the threading floor offered the space and the oxen for the burnt offering to David free of charge, but David retorted, *"No, but I will surely buy it from you for a price; nor will I offer burnt offerings to the LORD my God with that which costs me nothing" (v. 24).* David paid fifty shekels of silver for the space, which history attests to as the same place where Jesus paid the final price for the sin of mankind on the cross of Calvary. Was David's sacrifice accepted? Yes, it was. We know this to be true because the Bible says, *"So the LORD heeded the prayers for the land, and the plague was withdrawn from Israel" (v. 25).*

5. Keeping the temple of your body pure

Your body is the temple of God where the Holy Spirit resides, and therefore, must be kept pure. It is in your body that you make the sacrifice to God, and in addition to your motive and other conditions, your body must be well prepared for the reasonable service of offering sacrifice to God. The Bible says, *"I beseech you therefore, brethren, by the mercies of God, that you present your bodies a living sacrifice, holy, acceptable to God, which is your reasonable service" (Rom 12:1).* This is to say that your body must be presented to God as holy as you present your body in service to God. Paul admonishes that Christians must keep their bodies from the sin of fornication because while other sins are committed outside the body, fornication is committed against the body. Listen to what he said,

> *Flee sexual immorality. Every sin that a man does is outside the body, but he who commits sexual immorality sins against his own body. Or do you not know that your body is the temple of the Holy Spirit*

who is in you, whom you have from God, and you are not your own? ²⁰ For you were bought at a price; therefore glorify God in your body and in your spirit, which are God's (1 Cor 6:19-20).

There is no doubt that sacrifice is always acceptable to God if properly presented. This makes a sacrifice an essential aspect of prayer, and the highest level of prayer. When sacrifice goes up, blessings come down. Another aspect of sacrifice you should note is the fact that sacrifice is applicable to all other levels of prayer. For example, you could aid your prayer of asking, seeking, knocking, and all others with sacrificial offering. At every level of prayer, a sacrifice is applicable, and acceptable by God, if properly presented. For example, Cornelius was a man of prayer, but he did not just pray because the Bible says that he was always praying and giving alms to the poor. Thus, whatever kind of prayer he prayed was always aided by alms. This is why the angel testified that his prayer came to God as a memorial, and God remembered him.

Conclusion

There are usually two sides to prayer; the side of the person praying, and that of the One receiving the prayer. For prayer to be effective, the two sides must properly sync. Incidentally, it is only one side that is predictable and reliable. This is the side of the God who is receiving the prayer, while the side of the person praying is very unpredictable and unreliable. God who receives prayer does not change. The Bible says, *"Jesus Christ is the same yesterday, today, and forever" (Heb 13:8).* Therefore, knowing the character and attributes of God would normally make the person praying have a clear understanding of God's reaction to prayers; and with this, we could easily predict how He would react to prayers that fulfill certain conditions. God is faithful, reliable and dependable, and so also are His promises which are *"Yea and Amen" (2 Cor 1:20).* Also, there is no doubt that God answers prayer (see 1 Jn 5:14; Jere 33:3; 2 Chro 7:14; Jere 29:11).

Since prayer is inevitable, and there is no substitute to prayer, it is necessary to explore how the unpredictability of the person praying could be more rewarding. This is with a view to making prayer more productive and exciting than it used to be. Also, it is important to know that prayer is not optional, otherwise Jesus would have said, *"If you pray,"* and not *"When you pray"* (Matt 6:12). Therefore, it is the responsibility of the person praying to determine what kind of prayer the reliable and dependable God would attend to and what prayer He is not interested in. Also, it is the responsibility of the person praying to explore the principles of prayer based on the antecedents of prayer to determine how God reacted to certain prayers and why he reacted in such manner. It is in search of answers to these and other issues about prayer that I have come up with *The Seven Levels of Prayer.*

This is a practical book, and I encourage you to make the best use of it. All the steps are practical, and there are principles drawn out from the Scriptures, which could easily be applied in your prayer life because principles don't change. Whatever result are highlighted from the biblical examples would very much be the same result that are applicable if the same conditions are satisfied. I am sure that this book would be of great benefit to you as it is designed to make your prayer life more dynamic and exciting. By the application of the principles highlighted in this book, it is expected that the frustrations that have plagued your prayer life would be no more, but you would be able to take your prayer to the next level progressively. Thus, with this prayer experience, you would get to know that prayer is not a dead end phenomenon, neither is it a one-size-fits-all kind of spiritual exercise. Prayer is progressively dynamic. This Truth is expected to give you the confidence to step up your prayer for desired results.

I hope that as you explore the principles laid out in this book, your prayer life would change for the better, and every frustration that has been part of your prayer life would have no place any more. I hope too that your relationship with God would henceforth include your knowing God as a prayer-answering God. I pray you would henceforth begin to experience answers to your prayers. Amen.

Notes

1. Unger, Merrill. Unger's Bible Dictionary. 1961.
2. Monroe, Myles. *The Power and Purpose of Prayer.* Shippensburg PA: Destiny Image Publishing, 2000
3. Errico, Rocco and Lamsa George. *Aramaic Light on the Gospels of Mark and Luke.* Smyrna GA: Nohra Foundation. 2001.
4. Murdock, Mike. *The Law of Recognition.* Denton, Ft. Worth: TX. The Wisdom Center, 1999.
5. Ibid.
6. Willis, Arthur. *God's Chosen Fast.* London, Great Britain: Campton Printing Ltd. 1968.
7. Ibid.
8. Ibid.
9. Ibid.
10. Oxford Desk Dictionary. 1997

Prayers

Prayer of Asking and Receiving

Scriptural Confession:

At Gibeon the LORD *appeared to Solomon in a dream by night; and God said, "Ask! What shall I give you?"* [6] *And Solomon said: "You have shown great mercy to Your servant David my father, because he walked before You in truth, in righteousness, and in uprightness of heart . . .* [9] *Therefore give to Your servant an understanding heart to judge Your people, that I may discern between good and evil. For who is able to judge this great people of Yours? (1 Kings 3:5-9).*

If you then, being evil, know how to give good gifts to your children, how much more will your Father who is in heaven give good things to those who ask Him! (Matt 7:11).

And whatever you ask in My name, that I will do, that the Father may be glorified in the Son. [14] *If you ask*[c] *anything in My name, I will do it (Jn 14:13-14).*

You lust and do not have. You murder and covet and cannot obtain. You fight and war. Yet you do not have because you do not ask (Jms 4:2).

Prayer Guide

1. Thank God for all His blessings

2. Recognize God as the source of all blessings because every good and perfect gift comes from above.

3. O Lord my Father, I am asking that you perfect all the good things concerning me, for I ask in Jesus' mighty name.

4. Lord Jesus, let all my disappointment become divine appointment, in the name of Jesus

5. Lord Jesus, let all satanic words and storms be silenced in my life, in the name of Jesus

6. Father, I ask that you open fresh doors of prosperity unto me, in the name of Jesus

7. Lord, you said that I have the mind of Christ, I ask that you give me anointed ideas and lead me to new paths of blessing, in the name of Jesus

8. O Lord, I ask that you do something in my life that will change my life for good, in the name of Jesus

9. O Lord, I ask that every satanic limitation to my health and finances be removed, in the name of Jesus

10. O Lord, I ask that the spiritual anointing for breakthrough fall upon me, in the name of Jesus

Prayer for Open Heavens

Pray this prayer when it seems your heaven is shut up against you, and nothing is working well for you. Pray for a specific number of days with fasting, and give a sacrificial offering.

Scriptural Confession:
Now Jacob went out from Beersheba and went toward Haran. [11] So he came to a certain place and stayed there all night, because the sun had set. And he took one of the stones of that place and put it at his head, and he lay down in that place to sleep. [12] Then he dreamed, and behold, a ladder was set up on the earth, and its top reached to heaven; and there the angels of God were ascending and descending on it (Gen 28:10- 12).

Oh, that You would rend the heavens! That You would come down! That the mountains might shake at Your presence—(Isa 64:1).

Then he said to me, "Do not fear, Daniel, for from the first day that you set your heart to understand, and to humble yourself before your God, your words were heard; and I have come because of your words. [13] But the prince of the kingdom of Persia withstood me twenty-one days; and behold, Michael, one of the chief princes, came to help me, for I had been left alone there with the kings of Persia (Dan 10:12-13).

Prayer Guide:

1. Thank God for His protection over you and your family

2. Lord, let the power from above fall on me today to do the impossible, in the name of Jesus.

3. Lord, let every good and perfect gift from above locate me today, in the name of Jesus

4. I command the rain of abundance, goodness, favor, and mercy to fall on every area of my life, in the name of Jesus.

5. Lord, let divine glory from above overshadow my life, in the name of Jesus

6. O Lord, give me the key to good success so that anywhere I go, the door of good success will open to me, in the name of Jesus.

7. O Lord, let the anointing to excel in my spiritual and physical life fall on me, in the name of Jesus.

8. Let the power from above fall on me to do the impossible, in the name of Jesus

9. O Lord, let your favor and that of men encompass me today and always, in the name of Jesus.

10. O Lord, create in me a new heart by your power, in the name of Jesus.

11. O Lord, renew the right spirit in me, in the name of Jesus

12. I reject all that rob me of the joy of my inheritance in your kingdom, in the name of Jesus.

13. I speak to all evil mountains and break their power over my life, in the name of Jesus.

14. O Lord, enable me to hear your voice, in the name of Jesus

15. Lord, let me know your mind on every issue of my life, in the name of Jesus

16. Thank God for answered prayer

Prayer for Power to Prosper

It is God who gives the power to prosper, and therefore, to prosper, you must make it happen God's way. Make this your daily prayer because prosperity is not just in having money, but in enjoying all the blessings of God, some of which money cannot buy.

Support this prayer with a sacrificial offering.

Scriptural Confession:

> *They shall not be ashamed in the evil time, And in the days of famine they shall be satisfied.*
>
> *The young lions lack and suffer hunger; But those who seek the LORD shall not lack any good thing.*
>
> *And you shall remember the LORD your God, for it is He who gives you power to get wealth, that He may establish His covenant which He swore to your fathers, as it is this day (Deut 8:18).*
>
> *The LORD will guide you continually, And satisfy your soul in drought, And strengthen your bones; You shall be like a watered garden, And like a spring of water, whose waters do not fail (Isa 58:11).*

Prayer Guide:

1. I possess all my possessions, in the name of Jesus

2. I cover my hard work with the fire of God, in the name of Jesus

3. O Lord, put to shame every evil force that is against my inheritance, in the name of Jesus

4. Let every tree of profitless hard labor be uprooted in my life, in the name of Jesus.

5. O Lord, surprise me with abundance in every area of my life, in the name of Jesus.

6. Let the anointing for money-yielding ideas fall upon my life, in the name of Jesus

7. Father God, let all satanic hosts against my prosperity receive blindness and commotion, in the name of Jesus

8. Let all hindrances to my prosperity be destroyed by fire, in the name of Jesus.

9. I command all my caged blessings to be released and locate me by fire, in the mighty name of Jesus.

10. I reject the spirit of slavery and hardship in every area of my life, in the name of Jesus

11. O Lord, let my blessings begin to locate me from the North, South, East and West, in the name of Jesus.

12. Let the springs of joy fill my tabernacle all the days of my life, in the name of Jesus

13. O Lord, convert all my past failures to success, in the name of Jesus

14. Lord, prepare the table of blessings before me in the presence of my enemies, in the name of Jesus

15 For Christ has redeemed me from the curse of poverty and failure in life. therefore, I walk in total prosperity and success, in the name of Jesus

16. I decree that I will spend all my days in total prosperity and my years in great pleasure, in the name of Jesus

17. Thank God for answered prayer

Prayer to Break the Power of Darkness

When you experience the attack of the enemy in your sleep or in any area of your life, pray this prayer with fasting for a number of days, and give a battle seed offering.

Scriptural confession:
>*For there is no sorcery against Jacob, Nor any divination against Israel. It now must be said of Jacob And of Israel, 'Oh, what God has done! (Num 23:23).*
>
>*Christ has redeemed us from the curse of the law, having become a curse for us (for it is written, "Cursed is everyone who hangs on a tree"[h]), [14] that the blessing of Abraham might come upon the Gentiles in Christ Jesus, that we might receive the promise of the Spirit through faith (Gal 3:13-14).*
>
>*And they overcame him by the blood of the Lamb and by the word of their testimony, and they did not love their lives to the death (Rev 12:11).*
>
>*No weapon formed against you shall prosper, And every tongue which rises against you in judgment You shall condemn. This is the heritage of the servants of the LORD, And their righteousness is from Me," Says the LORD (Isa 54:17).*

Prayer Guide:

1. I cover myself and my family with the blood of Jesus

2. Lord, I receive the power to cast out devils according to your Word, and I command every witchcraft spirit tormenting me and my family to be cast out, in the name of Jesus.

3. O Lord my Father, preserve me from the wicked spirit and violent men that have positioned themselves to trouble me, in the name of Jesus

4. I command every power that operate in the water world, snake world, animal kingdom, and under the ground to turn against themselves, in the name of Jesus

5. Lord Jesus, I command every agent of witchcraft that despises my existence to bow at the soles of my feet, in the name of Jesus

6. Lord Jesus, you are the only God who delivers. I claim deliverance from every witchcraft spirit fighting against ,me, in the mighty name of Jesus.

7. Every mischief maker hindering my progress, let the horrible tempest stop your advancement in my life, in the name of Jesus

8. Lord Jesus, by your power, I come against all the kingdom of Satan releasing demons into my life, family and ministry to cease now. Let the fire of God completely raze them to ashes, in the name of Jesus

9. I decree that the forces of darkness will fail in their mission against me and my family, in the mighty name of Jesus

10. Lord Jesus, by the authority in your name, I break all the weapons of the enemy that are positioned against my life.

11. Every generational disgrace pursuing my family, I command you to stumble and catch fire.

12. Every stubborn and unrepentant demonic spirit contending with me, I overcome you with the blood of Jesus and I declare my freedom from all satanic bondages.

13. Lord Jesus, I now take a stand that I am a child of the light, and the darkness can never overcome me, in the name of Jesus

14. I take my place in the Word of God, and declare that He that is in me is greater than he that is in the world.

15. Father, I thank you for answered prayer, and for putting the devil to shame.

Prayer of Insistence and Persistence

Pray this prayer at every hour of prayer with fasting, and for a specific number of days, when you desperately need breakthrough in any area of your life. Also, support your prayer with a battle seed offering.

Scriptural Confession:
> *He did not waver at the promise of God through unbelief, but was strengthened in faith, giving glory to God, ^{21} and being fully convinced that what He had promised He was also able to perform.*

> *Surely the Lord GOD will help Me; Who is he who will condemn Me? Indeed they will all grow old like a garment; The moth will eat them up (Isa 50:9)*

> *The eternal God is your refuge, And underneath are the everlasting arms; He will thrust out the enemy from before you, And will say, 'Destroy!' Then Israel shall dwell in safety, The fountain of Jacob alone, In a land of grain and new wine; His heavens shall also drop dew Happy are you, O Israel! Who is like you, a people saved by the LORD, The shield of your help And the sword of your majesty! Your enemies shall submit to you, And you shall tread down their high places" (Deut 33:27-29).*

Prayer Guide:

1. Thank God for He alone is able to deliver and set free

2. In the name of Jesus, I release myself from spirit husband/wife, and let the blood of Jesus separate us permanently.

3. O Lord, I release myself from periodic disappointment and sorrow, in the name of Jesus

4. Lord Jesus, I destroy every form of parental curse placed on me consciously or unconsciously, in the name of Jesus

5. O God of new beginning, do a new thing in my marital life, and let every eye see it, in the name of Jesus

6. O Lord, my Father, I renounce every spirit of loneliness in my life, and I command it to cease, in the name of Jesus

7. Lord Jesus, let every garment of shame and reproach that the enemy has prepared for me catch fire, in the name of Jesus

8. In the name of Jesus, by the fire of the Holy Ghost, I reject every spirit of getting married in my dream, in the name of Jesus

9. O Lord, by the blood of Jesus, wash away my reproach.

10. O Lord. let every strange mark in my body be erased by the blood of Jesus

11. I reject every evil family pattern in the name of Jesus

12. You are the only God who can do what no man can do. Lord, do for me what the world said is impossible, in the name of Jesus

13. In the name of Jesus, every sexual sin troubling my life, I reject and renounce you, and I command you to leave me now, in the name of Jesus

14. My God and my Father, I shall receive my deliverance in this prayer program, in the name of Jesus

15. My God and my Father, I shall receive my joy instead of sadness in this prayer program, in the name of Jesus

16. My God and my Father, I shall receive my breakthroughs in this prayer program, in the name of Jesus

17. My God and my Father, I shall laugh last, in the name of Jesus

18. Worship God and thank Him for His provisions that can never fail. He has promised, and he will make it come to pass (Jer 1:12)

19. Confess all your sins to God and ask for forgiveness-- including those sins that you know could hinder your pregnancy. As you confess, make a vow that you will sin no more.

21. Thank God from your heart for what he has done and will do in your life

Prayer to Open the Book of Remembrance

Pray this prayer when you want God to show you uncommon favor before men, and give a sacrificial offering.

Scriptural Confession:
Who is he who speaks and it comes to pass, When the Lord has not commanded it? (Lam 3:37).

For the scepter of wickedness shall not rest On the land allotted to the righteous, Lest the righteous reach out their hands to iniquity (Ps 125:3).

"As for you also, Because of the blood of your covenant, I will set your prisoners free from the waterless pit. [12] Return to the stronghold, You prisoners of hope. Even today I declare That I will restore double to you (Zech 9:11-12).

And the Lord will deliver me from every evil work and preserve me for His heavenly kingdom. To Him be glory forever and ever. Amen! (2 Tim 4:18).

Prayer Guide:

1. Thank God for standing by His promise to fulfill it in your life.

2. O God, open your book of remembrance and locate me, in the name of Jesus

3. O God, open your book of remembrance assigned for my breakthrough now, in the name of Jesus

4. O God, open your book of remembrance for my uncommon blessing, in the name of Jesus

5. My God and my Father, draw me out by your mercy from the pit of forgetfulness that the enemy has put me, in the name of Jesus

6. Lord, let every book of disgrace and shame that the enemy has opened on my behalf, close by fire in the name of Jesus.

7. Lord, let every book of non-achievement that the enemy has opened on my behalf close by fire, in the name of Jesus.

8. Lord, let the book of favor and honor open on my behalf, in the name of Jesus

9. O Lord, let the book of remembrance that will make me celebrate my Samuel (blessings from God) open now, in the name of Jesus

10. O Lord, let the book of remembrance for my promotion be opened in the order of Modecai, in the name of Jesus.

11. O Lord, as you open the book of remembrance on my behalf, let all my forgotten blessings be released to me, in the name of Jesus.

12. You remembered Hannah, and her situation was turned around dramatically. O Lord, let my situation be turned around, no matter how hopeless it has been, as you open the book of remembrance for me, in the name of Jesus.

13 O God, open the book of remembrance for me, and let all my enemies know that you are the Lord who is able to take someone from the miry pit and set him up on the hill top.

14. O Lord, open the book of remembrance for me, and let my sorrow and sadness be turned to joy and happiness, in the name of Jesus

15. O Lord, open the book of remembrance for me, and let all my disappointments and failure be turned into success and blessings, in the name of Jesus.

Prayer of Vow

When you are struggling with a habit or lifestyle that is progressively destroying your life, and have taken every necessary step for your deliverance, pray this prayer of vow in support of your determination to be stay clean. Make the temple of your body clean, and give yourself as a living sacrifice.

Prayer Guide:

1. Thank God for His goodness and mercy for you and your family

2. O Lord of Heaven, I vow before you today that I will stay away from every form of sexual immorality that is capable of defiling me. Lord help me by your Spirit to be able to accomplish this vow, in the name of Jesus

3. O Lord of Heaven, I vow before you today that I will keep my body clean and holy from every form of sexual pollution that is capable of defiling me. Lord, help me by your Spirit to be able to accomplish this vow, in the name of Jesus.

4. O Lord of Heaven, I vow before you today that I will keep my mind pure from pornography that is capable of polluting my mind. Lord, help me by your Spirit to be able to accomplish this vow, in the name of Jesus.

5. O Lord of Heaven, I vow before you today that I will consistently study the Word of God for my enrichment. Lord, help me by your Spirit to be able to accomplish this vow, in Jesus' mighty name.

6. O Lord, destroy any oath or vow made secretly against me, in the name of Jesus.

7. O Lord, destroy any oath made secretly against my children, in the name of Jesus

8. O Lord of heaven, I vow before you today that I will keep away from any substance that can influence my mind negatively. Lord, help me by your Spirit to be able to accomplish this vow, in the name of Jesus.

9. O Lord of heaven, I vow before you today that I will keep away from any alcoholic drink that can pollute my mind and body. Lord, help me by your Spirit to be able to accomplish this vow, in the name of Jesus.

10. O Lord of heaven, if you will help me in my struggle against the habits that are ruining my life, I will serve you with my whole being, all the days of my life. Lord, help me to be able to accomplish this vow, in the name of Jesus

11. Lord, prepare me as a living sacrifice for you.

12. Give God prause for answered prayer

Contact Information

To order copies of this book, or if you need further prayer or counseling concerning any spiritual issue of your life, or if this book has been of benefit to you, and you want to share your testimony, contact us in any of the following ways:

Email: admin@licaim.org

www.licaim.org

Mail: 915 Woodland Trl, C4
       Smyrna GA, 30080

Phone: 678-508-6690

Made in United States
North Haven, CT
26 December 2022

30100489R00075